A Question of Leadership

Charles Grimes

To VIRGIL FOX
for years of inspiration.
Thank You

Published by: LBC Wise Counsel

ISBN 978-1-9160690-9-1

Copyright © 2019 Charles Grimes

British Library Cataloguing in Publication Data available.

Contents

Overture

Overture

"Leadership cannot be taught ...
but it can be learned!"

Peter Koestenbaum

So, another book on Leadership. Is this really what the world wants or needs? How can yet another volume be justified? As a subject, hasn't Leadership been done to death? Hasn't it been dissected and examined from every angle? Is there really anything else that can be said? After all, a quick search on Amazon will offer you thousands of titles, presumably enough to cover most eventualities? With all those ideas and all that scholarship deliverable at the mere click of a mouse, surely Leadership must be one of those areas that society has long since mastered.

But, of course, we haven't mastered it at all. We haven't even come close. As I write this early in 2019, with the US government in shutdown and the UK government in a Brexit stalemate it is clear that Leadership mastery – whatever that might mean or look like – is still a distant dream.

In this collection of essays I first want to offer some reflections on where we currently are and how we might have got here. I then want to explore where we might like our institutions and our organisations to move towards. And, finally, I'm going to take a look at some aspects of leadership – taking the lead, questioning and coaching, our abilities to listen, our approaches to change – that we might need to re-examine and re-assess to make this new journey possible.

Looking at the landscape ahead of us, we'll warm up with...

A QUARTET OF PRELUDES:

- Prelude 1 – Reflections on "What Is"
- Prelude 2 – Music and Musicians – a Leadership Metaphor
- Prelude 3 – Quotations
- Prelude 4 – What this book is not

The purpose of these four openers is both to establish some ground rules and also to assess the lay of the land. For example, throughout the book I make references to music. The first reason is simple: it's my passion in life. But there's another more important reason and that is that over the years I've become intrigued by connections between the two worlds of Music and Organisational Leadership. Many of the behaviours that I see organisations struggling with on a daily basis – teamwork, cross-functional collaboration, listening, change, creativity, consistency, responsibility, accountability, leadership and followership, engagement – these are challenges that professional musicians face as well. However, not only do they face them, but I would suggest that they're often better at overcoming them. I therefore want to explore whether some of the insights gained from the world of musicians might be transferable to the more traditional workplaces that most of us occupy.

WHERE ARE WE AND HOW DID WE GET HERE?

After this quartet of Preludes I'm going to explore where we are now and how we might have got here.

Whilst it's probably the fate of every generation to think that we're "going to hell in a handcart", this time around there's plenty of evidence to suggest that it's actually true! Many people believe that our organisations and institutions are dying, and that the "spiralling out of control" that we see around us are in fact cultural death-throes reminiscent of a buzzing fly on its last legs.

I want to examine briefly the context around contemporary leadership. How have we created our culture, one where we are all doing more and more of things that mean less and less? How has this happened? How have we got here? Is it just random chance, the way the dice have fallen? Or was it always going to happen? Could it, perhaps, have something to do with us, as creatures? Is there possibly a biological basis to this problem? Has it been, in some senses, an accident waiting to happen?

WHAT COULD OUR ORGANISATIONS LOOK LIKE?

After examining where we are organisationally and how we might have got here, I will then take a look at a promising alternative, a different organisational model, and consider how it might be more sustainable in the long term.

If the current world-view sounds depressing – and it undoubtedly is! – could it be better? Well, if we believe the activist, Satish Kumar "Whatever is created by humans can be changed by humans", maybe other possibilities and choices are available. What if we chose to see our organisations and institutions differently, perhaps as living systems, with cultures that honour connection and collaboration and wholeness? How might that new perspective affect how we see the organisation's purpose, its structure, how it manages itself, how it adapts and copes with change, not to mention how it engages with its employees?

THEMES AND VARIATIONS

Following this discussion of future possibilities we then come to a collection of thirty essays – Themes and Variations – in which I investigate various aspects of leadership that might help us on our journey. At first glance, the relevance of some of these essays may be hard to spot: they're not all obvious Corporate Leadership fayre. But each essay is accompanied by a number of Coaching Questions designed to ground the topic and to allow you to bring the essay into your particular world, to make it relevant to you.

You will also see that after each question there is space for you to capture any passing thoughts. The power of journaling has been well documented and I strongly encourage you to jot your ideas down. Of course, you don't have to and you may well be able to remember each and every one of your flashes of insight. But you probably won't. So, go on, write them down.

The thirty essays have been grouped into four broad categories or Themes:

Theme 1 – Leading

It seems that the time is ripe to ask some fundamental questions, challenge some basic assumptions, and take a fresh look both at what Leadership is and what it is not. Instead of using a reductionist "10 Secrets of Leadership"-style format, the approach will be less orthodox. At times I will examine the subject through a more philosophical lens and address questions such as What type of phenomenon is Leadership?, Is there a distinction between Leadership and Leaders?, and How do you study Leadership without sucking the life-force out of it, thereby killing it?

Theme 2 – Questioning

As the title of the book "A Question of Leadership" suggests, questions and questioning will be at its heart. But why are questions in general so powerful? What makes for a good question? Is there an art to asking questions? Why can it be difficult to ask questions? Do all questions have an answer? Is there ever a good or a bad time to ask a question? Which leadership questions do we need to rethink?

In this section we'll also take a look at the power of positive questioning via Appreciative Inquiry, a strengths-based enquiring approach to working with people that chooses to look for the positives. Imagine being asked by your boss questions such as … "What's working well?; What are your successes?; Give me examples of great teamwork, communication, influence, support, leadership that you've experienced here?". How might these positive, appreciative questions change your focus? How might they make you feel? How might they change the way you see the future? How might such questions open up and expand what is possible for you and your colleagues?

Theme 3 – Listening

From Appreciative questioning it's a short next step to Listening-to-the-answers. But what do we mean by listening? What do good listeners do? How can we improve our own personal listening? If we want to get better could we possibly learn to listen like an orchestral player or conductor? And what if we could broaden this skill to encompass our whole place of work? Might we be able to create a Listening Organisation? And what are the potential dangers if our organisations aren't listening?

Theme 4 – Changing

In many organisations Change is one of the most perplexing problems, almost insurmountably difficult. Vast sums of money are poured into all manner of "programmes" and "initiatives", with the hope that people – and therefore the organisation – will change. But, year after year, according to a 2017 article in the Harvard Business Review "About three-quarters of change efforts flop. Either they fail to deliver the anticipated benefits or they are abandoned entirely". Why is that? If it really is so difficult, do we perhaps need to view Change differently? Might it be that we're asking the wrong questions? Does Change really have to be arduous? Or can it be natural and organic? And what might the effects of that shift in perception be?

CODA – A REASON TO BE HOPEFUL

Looking to the future there are certainly plenty of reasons to be pessimistic. Wherever we look, problems abound. But, equally, there are significant and substantial reasons for optimism, the greatest being People.

Undoubtedly the most fundamental feature of being human is that our lives come to an end – as they say, "No-one gets out of this place alive." At a personal level this can be seriously depressing. But at the same time, the fact that we're finite, that we don't live forever, ensures the species' survival. It's death that enables humankind to adapt and change and thereby move forward.

The optimism that things can be better comes from the fact that, inexorably, the old guard perishes, the dinosaurs die. And a bright new generation comes forward, a generation bringing with it fresh ideas, new attitudes and ways of thinking, and a renewed energy. And that's a reason to be hopeful.

A Quartet
of Preludes

Prelude 1
REFLECTIONS ON "WHAT IS"

"The first responsibility of a leader
is to define reality."

Max De Pree

As the title suggests, this book is about Leadership. And it's also about the art of asking Questions. So, why the tagline "Reflections on What Is"? Well, the word "Reflections" hopes to convey several meanings. In one sense, these essays are simply jottings, personal musings on a range of subjects. Each reflection has a beginning, but at the same time they're all unfinished. They have no real endings. Because that's where you come in. The word "Reflections" also points towards what I want you, the reader, to derive from the book – and that is that my fledgling ideas and questions encourage you to create your own "Reflections" on leadership, coaching, change, listening, purpose, and so on. This process of "self-reflection", of "self-knowledge", of "looking in the mirror" is, of course, the very starting point of learning and developing,

And "What Is"? Well, it seems to me that this is one half of the most fundamental polarity that we all need to manage in our lives. Somehow we need to strike a balance between "What Should Be" (or "What we would like things to be") and "What Actually Is". And I don't think it's as easy as we make out.

One of the qualities that distinguishes us from other animals is our ability to go beyond our limitations, to exceed what we might initially think is possible. As humans, we are able to dream and imagine alternative futures for ourselves. And we're able to plan and make choices. This has been one of the keys to our success as a species, making us extraordinarily adaptable, and allowing us to colonise every part of the planet. Regardless of how hot or cold or wet or dry, humans have found a way to survive in almost every environment, in a way that no other single creature has.

But this ability to see possibilities, to see "what might be", can – like every other strength we have – become a weakness when overused, or perhaps even a delusion in extreme cases. Most of the time this is avoided because as well as our capacity for seeing "What might be", we also have a counter-balancing awareness of self, an ability for seeing "What is". Provided we keep the two roughly in balance then all is well. That goes for teams and organisations as a whole, as well as us as individuals.

Unfortunately, keeping the two in balance is not easy. To begin with, imagining how we would like things to be, dreaming about our futures, living in an imagined world of ideals is a lot more fun than shining a torch into the dark recesses of our lives and looking at how things actually are. When we look at What Is – really look at What Is – it's unsettling and uncomfortable. Instead of there being certainty, we have to admit to uncertainty, instead of clarity there is ambiguity, instead of simplicity we're surrounded by complexity. And whilst we can take some comfort in celebrating our strengths and the value we bring, at the same time we have to admit to and acknowledge our weaknesses, our frailties, our vulnerabilities, our fears. And that is hard, hard work.

Prelude 2
MUSIC and MUSICIANS ...
a LEADERSHIP METAPHOR

"Music is the universal language of mankind."

Henry Wadsworth Longfellow (attrib)

The Fabric of my Life

As I've already explained, there will be many references to music throughout the book. And the reason is simple: it's my passion in life. Music is what takes me to another level. For me, Music, in all its many guises, forms the backbone of my life, and is central to who I am. I have tunes going through my head almost all of the time. I hum sonatas and symphonies constantly, often to the annoyance of those around me. I've performed at a professional level for 50+ years (I started young!), and back in my 30s I earned my living in Classical Music broadcasting. As a result, I speak the language of music fairly fluently, and think of myself as "a musician". Music is the "fabric of my life", as the cellist, Steven Isserlis, once so tellingly described it.

And at the same time for the past 21 years I have earned my living in a different field, as a freelance Business Psychologist, helping individuals and groups in major organisations around the globe develop their leadership and management skills – teamwork, coaching, personal effectiveness, trust, influence, communication, decision making. As a result, over the years I've become intrigued by possible connections between these two worlds. Could some of the qualities and skills that I see and hear every day in highly trained musicians be transferable to the more traditional workplaces that most of us occupy?

Music and Organisational Leadership. What can they possibly have in common? The one is, stereotypically, artistic, expressive, creative, imaginative, passionate, emotive, intangible, spontaneous, idealistic: the other is concrete, boundaried, tangible, pragmatic, realistic, factual, step-by-step, grounded, commercial.

Two separate and distinct worlds with no Venn diagram-like overlap. Well, at first glance, maybe. But my suggestion is that when we look deeper then we see an altogether different and richer picture, one which shows multiple links and correspondences. And with this picture comes the opportunity to gain new perspectives and learnings about ourselves and others.

Ever since my early twenties I've been familiar with these two worlds. But to begin with I only saw "difference". When I looked at my musician-friends, and then observed colleagues in my then new workplace, these people were polar opposites, dissimilar in every respect. The world of Music – and especially Classical Music – seemed diametrically opposed to the organisation I then worked in. It was clear to me that Music represented all the artistic qualities listed above, whilst my organisation exemplified aspects of life that were more commercially oriented.

That's what I used to believe. Now? I'm not so sure.

Why Music is important to everyone

Before discussing the parallels between Music and Organisational Leadership it might be useful to take a look at why I believe music is important not just to me but to all of us. Why does it play such a central role in our lives?

In the outdoor and trekking world, there's a concept known as the Rule of Three, a simple guide suggesting how long an average person can survive in a harsh wilderness when deprived of the basics:

- 3 weeks without food
- 3 days without water
- 3 hours without shelter
- 3 minutes without air

Of course, it's an approximate guide, but it does make its point vividly – when it comes to the fundamentals of life, nothing comes close to air. It's the very stuff of our being. To imagine life without air is impossible. They are "as one". The two are completely inter-linked.

But let's think, for a moment, about music. Music is simply sound, organised sound. And sound fundamentally is air (or 'sonorous air' as the composer Busoni once remarked). Music is nothing more than moving air particles. Without air, music is impotent. To imagine music without air is impossible. They, too, are "as one", completely interlinked. Air and Life … Air and Music. Could it be that, like air itself, Music is fundamental to us all as individuals? In fact, could it be that it's part of our history, our ancient history?

Despite the importance of speech to modern man, it's worth remembering that for most of our 500,000 year past we haven't used words to get by: we've communicated perfectly adequately without spoken language. The ability to create verbal language – a skill which requires us being able to manipulate sophisticated symbols – didn't arrive until relatively recently. It may have started to develop about 80,000 years ago but is more likely to have been closer to 40,000 years ago. So, this begs the question: What were early-humans doing prior to this time? If they weren't using words, then how were they communicating for the previous 400,000+ years?

The ability to speak relies not only on a specific type and level of intelligence but also on being able to create a controlled flow of air over the vocal cords, being able to control the breath. This is a skill that is surprisingly rare. For example, whilst our closest relatives, the primates, might possibly have the necessary intelligence to create speech, they're not actually able to control their breath and phrasing, and they can't modulate the intonation of the sound well enough to create speech. They simply don't possess the necessary vocal apparatus to do this, and this is one reason that attempts to teach apes to talk have met with so little success thus far.

By comparison, when we look at early-humans the fossil evidence suggests that even 400-500,000 years ago they had developed a vocal apparatus comparable to modern humans and so were capable of creating sustained sounds. At the same time, although they were social creatures who obviously communicated between each other, we know that what we might call 'speech' was not present. The suggestion, therefore, from a number of anthropologists is that early-Humans communicated through a sort of non-verbal language, a "musi-language", one in which there was intonation and phrasing, but no actual words; in essence, a rudimentary form of Music, just as we see with various species today – from canaries to whales.

This importance of music can be further seen when we look at how language has developed in more recent times. In literature it's interesting that poetry, which relies so much on the musical aspects of words, developed before prose. And if we consider how language develops in each of us as individuals, it's worth noting that although as adults we eventually become extremely visual creatures, we start out as aural ones – foetuses in the womb start to hear from Day 45 whereas the eyes of a baby are not properly developed till many weeks after birth. It's not surprising therefore that when we communicate with new-borns, our "baby talk" instinctively focuses on the overall sound, the musical elements (pitch, rhythm, intonation), sounds to which the baby has been attuned for months.

Have musicians found the Holy Grail?

After several decades with my feet in both camps, the similarities and parallels between the worlds of Music and Organisations seem abundantly clear. Actually, this shouldn't be that surprising.

"Organisations", after all, are no more than groups of people. And so it doesn't much matter whether that group is creating new Pharmaceutical products, solving complex Legal problems, developing cutting-edge Software programmes, or playing Beethoven symphonies. Whenever you get a collection of individuals working together there is the potential to create something truly remarkable. And, at the same time, there is the capacity for the whole enterprise to implode under a cloud of acrimony and bad feelings.

By and large, performing musicians manage to avoid implosion whilst at the same time creating magic. It is my proposition, therefore, that somehow they have stumbled across the corporate Holy Grail – a way to create results of the highest quality by working together as a unit. It's a big claim, I know, but I am convinced there are things that people in organisations – for the purposes of these essays I will call them "Non-musicians" – can learn from their "Musician" counterparts, and it's my intention to explore these in the coming pages.

It seems to me that many significant challenges faced by teams of Non-musicians are just everyday hurdles for groups of musicians.

- *Excellence* – how to move from Good to Great and accept only outstanding performance

- *Perseverance* – being prepared to put in the thousands of hours of mundane work to achieve fleeting moments of magic

- *Consistency* – being able to produce your best results every day, every week, every month

- *Pressure* – performing when you're fearful, when it matters, when the stakes are high

- *Listening* – to others and yourself with ruthless attention and honesty in search of the truth

- *Collaboration* – truly working with colleagues as a team rather than as a group

- *Delegation* – the orchestral conductor delegating everything, and becoming the one person on stage who makes no sound

- *Creativity* – imagining and creating something magical from a set of black dots on a page

- *Change* – making constant adjustments and corrections to your behaviours so as to blend with those around you

- *Responsibility* – taking the lead and individually stepping up to the plate with confidence and certainty of purpose

- *Followership* – knowing when to take on a supportive role and let others take the lead

- *Authority* – how to direct people who know more and are more expert than you

- *Self-management* – discovering and developing leadership in a leader-less team

- *Feedback* – cultivating trust so as to be able to give and receive feedback

- *Perceptions* – being able to accept and embrace the validity of someone else's view

- *Commitment* – being prepared to trust in your abilities, to take risks and "go for it"

Whilst these are often real headaches in the organisational world, they're all taken for granted by performers in orchestras, choirs and chamber groups. It's simply what they do. It's how they live their life.

Listening, for example, is what music is about. That what it teaches you. As a musician you can't NOT listen, just like an artist can't NOT observe. That's what you do. Hence my belief that there are many learnings that can be transferred.

Prelude 3
QUOTATIONS

"Misquotations are the only quotations
that are never misquoted."

Hesketh Pearson

Throughout the book I've used various quotations. But, before we start, I must flag up the problem of Authorship. The provenance of some quotations is easy to verify, but others are just the opposite. In the age of the internet and Fake News, whilst it's infinitely easier than it once was to find a suitable quote, actually pinning down who wrote it is far trickier.

If we believe every quote to be genuine then we soon find that certain writers have been impossibly prolific. It's rather like the ubiquitous locks of Napoleon's hair that grace every museum known to man. Are all of these genuine? If they are then then he must have grown hair like Rapunzel. Likewise, there are certain historical figures who apparently commented on every possible topic, so much so that after a while you do wonder what is real and what is not.

Oscar Wilde and Mark Twain are favourites if the quote is remotely humorous, whilst Henry Ford and Albert Einstein are commonly cited when a quote needs a bit more weight. Maybe these people did say everything that is attributed to them, but it's probably more a case of Chinese Whispers, with the result that, as the decades pass by, these sayings simply become part of our folk-lore.

For me, authorship can at times be a distraction. For example, some music scholars question whether JS Bach actually did write 'his' famous Organ Toccata and Fugue in D minor. And, for decades, literary academics have been asking "Did Shakespeare write all his own plays, or were they penned by Marlowe or Bacon or some other contender?" Who knows? And does it matter to most of us? Is it important who put the marks on the page? Surely the bigger point is: Does this piece of music or these words speak to me, do they raise my spirits, and do they help me learn something about what it means to be human?

With regard to the quotes in this book I'm by no means certain who wrote every one of them, hence the word "attrib" after the names of some of the supposed authors. Personally, whether the words were penned by Abraham Lincoln or Voltaire or Longfellow frankly doesn't matter in the great scheme of things. I'm more interested in the sentiments conveyed by the quotes.

Prelude 4
WHAT THIS BOOK IS NOT

To avoid any misunderstandings, from the outset let's be clear about what this book is not.

It's not a Recipe Book

It most definitely is not a Recipe Book or a How-To guide. Naturally, such books have good intentions and their authors mean well. But they always leave so many things unsaid. If you've ever attempted a dish from a Cook Book and been frustrated that the end result doesn't look or taste quite as mouth-watering as it should, then you'll know what I mean. Yes, you used all the correct ingredients. And yes, you measured them meticulously. And yes, you followed the timings precisely. So, it should work and be an exact replica.

But it never is. Because a recipe, however detailed, can only ever be an approximation, a guide to what you do. No recipe mentions everything. Not only can it never capture that 'Delia Magic', but it also can't know how your cooker compares with Jamie's, or whether you've got the same brand of pots and pans that Heston uses in the Fat Duck. Not to mention subtleties like the weather and the altitude of your kitchen, both of which can have a significant effect on temperatures and boiling points.

So, this definitely is not a detailed recipe book to be followed slavishly. At best, it is a list of various ingredients. Some may be immediately appealing and relevant and give you fresh ideas. Others may be less so. Either way, whatever you do with them is up to you.

It's not a comprehensive, encyclopaedic guide

As I've explained, the book is simply a collection of essays which

I hope will give you some food for thought and get you asking questions. It's by no means a comprehensive guide to the subject, so it's more than likely that your pet topic will be missing. Sorry.

Even more infuriating, there will be no ready-made Answers. And "Universal Truths" will be thin on the ground, too.

What I want more than anything is to help you clarify what Leadership means to you. Any conclusions I might have drawn about the subject are completely useless to you. What you need to establish and be clear about are your conclusions.

It's not a "Cure-all"

It should go without saying – though I'll say it anyway, just to avoid any confusion – that these ideas will not solve all your problems. There are no universal remedies, no cure-alls in the field of Leadership, or any other field for that matter. No metaphor will fit every situation or every organisation. All models and frameworks are situational to some degree, all both "useful" and "useless" at different times. Your skill as a Leader is knowing When … when a model can help you, and when not. All the various Leadership models that exist are simply "lenses" through which you can examine organisational life. The more you have at your disposal, the greater your ability to create a picture with richness and depth and colour.

The search for any one single Leadership model is always futile because though it will offer you some "solutions", unfortunately these solutions are not the ones to your problem. Instead, they are the answers to someone else's problem, namely those of the author of the book! In the end, therefore, there can only ever be one way to go, and that's Yours. Yes, seek out thoughts and ideas from others. But finally, it's down to you.

So, with that said, let's get to it.

Where are we... and how did we get here?

WHERE ARE WE ...
AND HOW DID WE GET HERE?

"What a terrible era in which
idiots govern the blind."

William Shakespeare – Julius Caesar

Before we can study some of the details of Leadership and the other associated themes outlined in the Overture, we first need to examine the wider picture. Leadership doesn't exist in a vacuum. There is always a context. And, so, first we need to take a brief look at the state of leadership in the world that we see around us. When we watch the News on TV or read a newspaper what are some examples of leadership in the political or commercial worlds that we might have seen in recent times?

Politics is always an easy target. For centuries it has offered up a rich parade of figures who prefer self-interest to having a strong moral compass. But even against such stiff competition from history, US President Donald Trump and Russian President Vladimir Putin are still able to stand out. Trump clearly has some extraordinary skills. In the 2016 election he appealed to over 63 million voters – no mean feat in itself – and earlier in his campaign, in order to gain the Presidential nomination, he had to ward off challenges from 16 other Republican candidates. When the slug-fest was over he was "the last man standing". Putin is equally strong and resilient, as shown by his ability to stay at the top for almost two decades – he's been either President or Prime Minister of Russia since the year 2000. But at the same time, it would be hard to find two men who care less about their fellows, two men who are less compassionate, two men who are less sincere and trustworthy. It's as if they've both been created as Comic Book Baddies who crave nothing else but power; cartoon characters who thrive on throwing their weight around and getting what they want through School Bully tactics.

Not that the UK is faring much better when it comes to leadership. Ever since David Cameron, the then Prime Minister, absolved himself and his party of all political responsibility and instead called for a referendum on the UK's membership of the EU – what an impressive piece of leadership that was – the country has become obsessed by Brexit. Meanwhile, as deadlines for leaving the EU come and go, instead of working together and negotiating this staggeringly complicated "Divorce agreement" the Conservative and Labour parties have raised political infighting to an art form, rendering the country seemingly rudderless. With Theresa May dispatched to the political waste bin, the country next woke up to a new Prime Minister, Boris Johnson, who in his opening two months in office managed to lose his first six Commons votes, break the law by suspending Parliament, and mislead the monarch. It is little wonder that the UK was recently compared to "a dead fly in an emptying bath, spinning aimlessly as it heads towards the plughole".

A tale of Corporate greed

> "Earth provides enough to satisfy every man's needs,
> but not every man's greed."
>
> *Mahatma Gandhi (attrib)*

But even if the political world has its faults, at least the world of Commerce is in safe hands, isn't it? Presumably effective Leadership is alive and well in the Boardroom? In any well-run organisation we hope that the most senior executives are there to ensure the prosperity of the company, as well as their fellow employees and their customers. Surely this is a quality of all who get to the very top? Might we ever see examples of self-interest, of feathering-ones-own-nest? Well, step forward Jeff Fairburn, ex-CEO of

Persimmon Homes, a FTSE-100 UK house builder. In December 2017, as a result of having "worked very hard", he stood to benefit from a well-negotiated bonus scheme to the tune of more than £100 million. When that figure caused a public and Shareholder outcry he magnanimously agreed to a reduction and to accept a mere £75 million, presumably hoping that would be the end of the matter. But it wasn't. Government then got involved, with representatives of Persimmon being summoned to appear before the Business, Energy and Industrial Strategy Committee. Even when the committee Chair described Executive pay at Persimmon as "a tale of corporate greed" Jeff Fairburn was undimmed in his belief that the bonus of £75 million should be in his pocket rather than those of his fellow employees or clients. Legally he was, of course, "in the right": contractually, the bonus was his. But, was he "in the right" morally? What distorted version of Leadership justifies such "corporate greed", such self-interest?

With Persimmon Homes the "corporate greed", though morally questionable, was all perfectly legal. Other situations are simply not. They're criminal. And they can be on a scale that is truly breath-taking. Let's take the sorry tale of the Volkswagen Emissions scandal – or "Dieselgate" as it's affectionately known. For the past several decades reducing vehicle emissions has been on the To Do list of most governments. Not surprisingly, this is not popular with car manufacturers: reducing emissions is both expensive and bad news for the vehicles' performance. In the face of ever more stringent emissions rules VW came up with a novel solution to passing the testing procedures. It developed, created and installed software which would enable the cars to know when they were being tested and would then activate their emissions controls specially for the laboratory testing. This "cheat" conveniently caused the vehicles' Nitrous Oxide output to temporarily meet standards and therefore pass regulatory testing. However, as soon as the test was over the emissions controls were inactivated. Whilst this was good for the performance of the car, it meant that back on the road in the real-world the very same engine could emit up to 40 times more Nitrous

Oxide than it had done just moments earlier in the laboratory.

How had this happened? Early on in the scandal it was tempting to think that there might be a simple explanation. After all, in a company the size of VW with more than 100,000 employees there is always the potential for there being a "rogue engineer", a solo-operator who decides to venture off-piste. But then it emerged that this software had been installed not just in one or two cars, but in – wait for it! – eleven million vehicles. Yes, Volkswagen deployed this programming software in about eleven million cars worldwide, including 500,000 in the United States, from 2009 through 2015. This was cheating, as they say, on an industrial scale.

It raises so many questions about Leadership: How could the Executive team ever have imagined this was a good idea? What happened to the moral compasses of those in the team? How could the Board possibly have countenanced such behaviour? (And please, if the Board suggest they didn't know, well Why didn't they know? That's their role). Then there are the questions about organisational culture: Every engineer in VW would have known that something is not right; and yet nothing was said or heard. What does that say about the VW culture? Certainly, it was an environment where "bad news" didn't travel upwards, and "whistle-blowers" were not welcomed.

Sadly, these are not isolated cases. I could have picked dozens more. Barely a week goes by without some form of scandal, and they come from every sector – from Banking to Newspapers, from Retail to IT, and so on. But how have we got here? How have we created a society where the CEO of a house-building company thinks he is entitled to a £100 million bonus because he "worked very hard". How have we created a society where a company as famous and trusted as Volkswagen will do almost anything to achieve results, and thinks it is perfectly acceptable to lie and cheat. How have we created a society where in the years leading up to the financial crash of 2008 US Banks thought it was justifiable to sell mortgages to unsuspecting people who had no ways of repaying the loans because they had no jobs, no incomes, and no assets – the infamous NINJA Mortgages? How did ordinary employees in these organisations come to see such customers as fair game?

"It's human nature ... a Dog-eat-Dog world ... a Jungle out there" Our thoughts create our reality

Our ways of thinking, our belief systems, our assumptions about the world, our mental models, they all affect the version of reality we create for ourselves. I once attended a Sales conference hosted by an Insurance company where the theme for the event was "It's a Jungle out there". It's not hard to see where the organisers were coming from on this one. Clearly they were hoping to promote certain qualities and behaviours amongst their Sales force – that in a world where there are clearly Winners and Losers, that we had better be one of the very few Winners, and therefore we need to reward competitiveness, boldness, courage, strength, drive, assertiveness, purpose, challenge, determination. All of which are admirable. But what about qualities and behaviours such as collaboration, support, help, care, sensitivity, co-operation, compassion, harmony, kindness? These are equally admirable qualities and are also essential to the long-term sustainability of any group or team or organisation or indeed any client relationship. But are they likely to come to the fore and to be valued at an event entitled "It's a Jungle out there"? Our thoughts (and words) create our reality.

As with that Insurance company, where its values are plain to see, it's equally easy to see the reality that some individuals inhabit. As Freud commented "We leak the truth" every time we open our mouths. In effect, we give ourselves away. I was chatting to a London cabbie recently about money and inequality and large bonuses. His response was simple: "It's human nature, mate. Self-interest. You've got to look after #1". Well, yes. I suppose there are times when you must. If I were ever to find myself splashing around on the Titanic I suspect I may well push others aside and be tempted to "look after #1". But, more generally, isn't there also a place in our lives for compassion and kindness and altruism? I suggested to the cabbie that these are also part of human nature. "Yeah, but have you never watched David Attenborough? it's a Dog-eat-Dog world. Survival of the fittest. It's all about competition." As it happens, I have seen plenty of footage of unfortunate gazelles being brought down by cheetahs. It can be a brutal world. There are times when there are clear winners and losers. Competition certainly exists. But I've also seen enough programmes to know that the natural world is actually founded far more on collaboration than it is on competition, and that whilst "hunter .v. hunted" scenes of crocodiles and wildebeest make gripping TV, they are the exception rather than the rule. Nature is full of symbiotic relationships. Collaboration and co-operation are central to our lives as animals, and yet they can all too easily be seen as soft and as signs of weakness. In our League of Behaviours why have some behaviours been promoted to the Premiership while others have been relegated to League 2? What mindset has caused this? In short, how have we ended up with so many organisations and institutions that benefit a handful of people at the expense of the vast majority?

The MASTER and his EMISSARY

In his award-winning book, "The Master and his Emissary", Iain McGilchrist offers us what I believe are some possible clues, indeed, a very persuasive explanation. This book, which is sub-titled "The Divided Brain and the Making of the Western World", explores the question: Might the very structure of our brains have affected the world that we have created? Might the organisations and the institutions that we see around us, together with the underlying belief systems and mental models that we all use, have their roots in our own biology?

We all know that our brains are in two halves – that's been common knowledge for several thousand years. More recently, as a result of popular science literature, we've also come to talk about the "Right

Brain" and the "Left Brain", and we often ascribe certain functions to these two "brains". I'll come back to these claims shortly. But first, I want to return to McGilchrist's starting point, which for him was asking the question "WHY is the brain in two halves?" This is an important question, because it's not simply human brains that are structured in this way. In fact, the brains of all birds and animals take this form. Why would this be? What possible Darwinian advantage could be gained? And, moreover, why would the brain, which is all about making connections, have become increasingly disconnected, increasingly divided as human evolution has progressed? Why has the Corpus Callosum – that part of the brain that actually connects the two halves – got relatively smaller over time? And why is the main function of the Corpus Callosum not to enable communication but to actually inhibit it? Clearly it seems very important that the two halves of the brain be kept separate.

Whilst we all know about there being two hemispheres, perhaps less well known is the fact that the two halves are not symmetrical. The left and right hemispheres are shaped differently. This is odd. If the body simply needed a bigger brain and more brain capacity – ie: processing power – then you'd expect the brain would have developed symmetrically. The fact that it hasn't suggests that the two halves may be doing rather different things.

What might these be? Well, let's consider the idea of "attention", and our need to attend to the world in two very different ways. McGilchrist explains it this way. Imagine a small bird. In order to remain alive it needs to do two things – feed and stay safe – and these require very different types of attention. To eat, the bird must be able to focus its attention very narrowly and in a detailed way on a nourishing speck of food – ie: something it already knows – and it must be able to select it against a background of inedible grit. To stay safe, on the other hand, requires a very different type of attention. Whilst it is focusing on the speck of food, on what is familiar, the bird must also take in and observe the wider world where predators may be lurking. If it doesn't then there is a real danger of it becoming a meal for someone else. Thus, in order to survive, we need to attend to the world in two diametrically opposed ways. We need to see both the Whole and the Details simultaneously, "What is known" and "What is unknown", both at the same time. These are so profoundly different that we actually need two brains, or at least two connected hemispheres for survival.

It's about HOW not WHAT

So, the two hemispheres are different. But – and this is important, very important – they DO the same things. Both hemispheres help us attend to the world. The differences lie not in WHAT they do but rather HOW they do it. This is very different from what popular science led us to believe in the 1960s. Back then we were told that one part of the brain did Reason and the other did Emotion. That's now known to be false. Both hemispheres are involved in both Reason and Emotion, although in different ways. We were also told that most of Language was in the left hemisphere while Vision was in the right. Once again, that's false. It's much more complicated. It's now recognised that pretty much every aspect of our behaviour uses both hemispheres. The differences lie in the type of attention which each side gives us. The right hemisphere provides sustained, broad, open, vigilant attention, which allows us to understand and relate to the world. The left hemisphere, on the other hand, provides narrow, sharply focused attention to detail, which allows us to manipulate the world to our advantage

These types of attention apply to all animals. But we humans have an additional feature in our brains – the frontal lobes – whose function is to inhibit the rest of the brain. This gives us a certain amount of control over our instincts and allows us to stop "the immediate" happening. This in turn lets us stand back in time and space and see things from a distance, to see and understand "the other".

This distance is profoundly creative for everything that is human: it helps us empathise and create bonds with others, and it also allows us to manipulate and use the world around us (both for ill and good!). Furthermore, our left hemispheres enable us to "grasp" things, whether those things are tangible (such as tools) or intangible (such as concepts in language). When we want to articulate an idea precisely it's our left hemisphere that we use.

Another aspect of the left hemisphere is its ability to simplify, to "sort the wheat from the chaff". In this way we use it to create maps and mental models. Of course, these maps are not "reality": they are not "the whole". They just show key elements that we already know and deem to be important and useful, with all other extraneous information being omitted. Maps are simplified depictions of reality, but very useful all the same, enabling us to interact with and manipulate the world.

Whilst the left hemisphere likes simplified maps, the right hemisphere sees the whole, sees things in their entirety, and things in context rather than being separate. The right also prefers newness. It's always looking out for the unknown, for what we don't know, for what we're not expecting, for what doesn't fit. It sees connections and therefore uses metaphor. It understands implicit meaning, body language, facial expression. It deals with an embodied world, and understands individuals, not just categories. By contrast with the left hemisphere (which sees everything in a very reductionist and mechanistic way, with the whole being merely a "sum of its constituent parts") the right hemisphere prefers the living to the mechanical.

In essence, the left hemisphere operates in a closed system, where "perfection" is attainable. It provides us with clarity, and the power to grasp and manipulate things that are known, fixed, static, isolated, explicit, decontextualized and generalised. But the price of that is that the world it creates is ultimately lifeless and empty.

The right hemisphere, by contrast, operates in an open system, one where things are never fully graspable or perfectly known. It sees a living world, one which is full of individual, changing, evolving, interconnected, living beings.

So what?

So, OK, all very interesting. But, so what? What does any of this have to do with contemporary Politics, Corporate irregularities, or Leadership in general? Well, now that we have a better idea about how the two hemispheres operate and the views of the world that they offer us, we can now consider how we currently combine them, and how we have combined them historically. Are the two hemispheres always equally dominant? Over the centuries has it generally been 50/50? Or has the pendulum ever swung one way or the other, thus giving one hemisphere a cultural advantage? And where might we be now in the early 21st century?

Iain McGilchrist argues that during the fifteen hundred years, from Roman times up to the 15th/16th centuries in Europe, whilst there were small swings of the pendulum this way and that, there was overall a form of balance between the two hemispheres. However, he further argues that during the last five hundred years or so the pendulum has swung further and further towards the left hemisphere being dominant, leading to a modern world that is now profoundly out of balance. We now live in a world where a certain way of thinking has triumphed, where everything is reduced to the agenda of the left hemisphere. The problem with this is that the left hemisphere literally doesn't see what it doesn't see, and this results in us "not seeing" what the world is telling us, not experiencing the totality of life. It's a mindset which teaches that the only thing that matters is "utility", a mindset that focuses on "resources". It makes us very good at grabbing and grasping, but not very good at understanding. It's made us no wiser, or helped us understand what we're here for, or what it means to "be". We seem to have lost sight of the fact that everything that is truly valuable to us as humans can NOT be pursued or grasped or collected like chattels.

Neither has this approach helped us come to terms with the paradoxical and inconsistent nature of life. As we've seen the Left hemisphere loves maps, models, simplification. It therefore goes without saying that it seeks "consistency" – eg: one of the goals in Physics is to find a Theory Of Everything, a single, all-encompassing, coherent theoretical framework that fully explains and links together all physical aspects of the universe. The assumption behind this goal is that there must be some underlying consistency to the universe, which is what the Left hemisphere expects and, indeed, craves. But is there? Why should there be consistency?

Compared with the Left, the Right hemisphere is more comfortable looking at "what is" and accepting the notions of paradox and inconsistency. The Left hemisphere, on the other hand, faced with a choice between "what I see" and "what I would like to see" chooses NOT to reconcile and synthesise the two views but instead to ignore the former and focus on the latter.

The effects of the imbalances in the world, of our skewed thinking, are evident all around us. We seek happiness – "I just want my children to be happy" is what every parent says – and yet as a society we are profoundly un-happy as shown by ever-increasing levels of mental illness. Culturally, we've pursued freedom, and yet here in the UK we've ended up with our every step being monitored by CCTV cameras, and the data of our lives being in the possession of Amazon, Facebook and the like. And what happens to all this data? As each year passes we have more and more information to hand, and yet we become no wiser.

The left hemisphere world

I must stress that I am not criticising the left hemisphere at all. In no way is it bad! There is nothing wrong with what the left hemisphere has to offer. In fact, in an age like ours where language is used imprecisely (think Donald Trump) and there is a lack of reasoned thinking (think Populism and the mistrust of experts) then it becomes all the more important as a check. However, the left hemisphere must know its place. It must understand its role. It's there to help and support: But, since it doesn't see the "whole", it cannot lead. According to Einstein "the Rational mind is a faithful servant." The problem we have in contemporary society is that for far too long we have honoured the servant at the expense of the Master. This has been a very bad course of action and we are now paying the price.

Our modern world looks awfully like what we might imagine a "left hemisphere world" to be. We prioritise the virtual over the real – we've probably all seen groups of diners in a restaurant, each of whom is scrolling through stuff on their smart phone whilst ignoring the friends sitting directly in front of them. We surround ourselves with Technology – how many people do you know who don't own at least one of the following: a PC, laptop, iPad, tablet, smartphone? I'm guessing no-one, because we've all convinced ourselves that this "stuff" is essential, even though a mere thirty years ago no-one in the world had one and we all managed to get by OK. We see paranoia all around us – whether it be about Mexican immigrants, terrorists, refugees, inflation, the unemployed, or any other of a thousand potential "dangers". There's a belief that we need to govern and control everything, and so we see Bureaucracy, with all its strangling rules, flourishing. But this bureaucracy fails to control, and so we end up with a society that is ever-more fragmented, where there is a "lack of joined-up thinking", where "the right hand doesn't know what the left hand is doing"! (or should that be "hemisphere"?)

A world based on utility, on the material, on grasping and having, on achievement, on getting things done, on quantity, on self-interest, on the virtual, on separateness, on lifeless technology, on bureaucratic control, on fear and paranoia is not, on the face of it, very attractive. And yet, we've come to accept it and believe it's "the norm". Why? Because the left hemisphere is very convincing. It's good at simplifying (remember how it likes maps), and it's comfortable being selective and omitting material that doesn't fit its view. Its arguments are clear and straightforward, and they seem to "make sense". There is a self-consistency. Not only that, but the left hemisphere is also very articulate and vocal. The right hemisphere, by contrast, is far less vocal, and less capable or willing to construct arguments that pin things down. (How often have we heard someone say about a feeling "I can't find the words to describe it"?).

So, this is how things are. These are the values our contemporary society espouses. And they are reflected in our organisations and institutions. But do things have to remain this way? Could there be an attractive alternative? That's what we're going to explore next.

What could our Organisations and Institutions look like?

Future Possibilities

"The future interests me:
I'm going to spend the rest of my life there."

Mark Twain (attrib)

There's an idea in psychology known as negativity bias. It suggests that, comparatively speaking, we're far more affected by negative experiences than positive ones. It seems that things of a more negative nature – unpleasant thoughts, emotions, social interactions, traumatic events – have a greater effect on our psychological state than neutral or positive things. Something very positive tends to have less of an impact on our behaviour than something equally emotional but negative. This bias seems to affect a whole range of aspects of our lives – what we're drawn to; the way we attend to the world and learn; the way we make decisions and assess risk; the way we make sense of the world around us.

We see this bias in our News media. In 2014, two Canadian researchers, Marc Trussler and Stuart Soroka, conducted an experiment in which they used eye-tracking technology to see which articles people chose to read. The results demonstrated fairly clearly that the News stories that people were drawn to, the ones that were read most often, tended to be depressing ones. Participants in the experiment often chose stories with a negative tone – ones about corruption, set-backs, wrong-doings and so on – rather than neutral or positive stories. Interestingly, the people taking part in the experiment all claimed that they actually preferred good news, and that the media was too focused on negative stories. That's what they said. But their actions told a different truth, which is that people who are interested in current affairs and politics are most likely to choose the bad news stories.

This bias is probably a useful defence mechanism. It reminds us of the dangers, big and small, that constantly surround us. Looking for what has or could go wrong is a pretty good way of protecting ourselves. We have sayings such as "learn from our mistakes" and "once bitten, twice shy". These maxims make perfect sense. Reading about doom-and-gloom, about a dangerous world "out there" can help us feel safe. Most of the time, where we are is a warm, comfy, cosy place to be. But maybe it can be too cosy, too much of a protection. As with any protective gear that we might wear, this psychological bias can weigh us down and restrict our movements. It can get in our way, and suddenly, the cure is worse than the disease, the side-effects of the remedy are worse than the initial problem.

As we will see in a later essay, noticing this negativity mindset provided the stimulus for David Cooperider's Doctoral thesis, the one that eventually gave rise to Appreciative Inquiry. Right at the start of his studies he found that way more than 90% of the academic papers relating to Organisational Development that were already available focused on a "deficit discourse" – ie: what's wrong, what's not working, what's missing, what's failing in our organisations. Whilst these deficits are important to be aware of and must be acknowledged, a deficit discourse stifles creativity and imagination, weighs people down and overpowers "possibility thinking". In short, it's suffocating.

Something new, waiting to be born

But times are changing. For several decades now, writers as diverse as Alvin Toffler in "Future Shock", Fritjof Capra in "The Turning Point", and Iain McGilchrist in "The Master and his Emissary" have been describing and illuminating past societal changes, and outlining a range of potentially more positive futures.

When we're in the middle of change – personal, organisational or societal – it can seem slow, even glacial. That's because change is rarely a straight line steadily moving upwards. Change is much more incremental. Anyone who has ever tried to develop a new skill, say learning to play a musical instrument or kick a football, will have experienced this. The practice is done very assiduously, day after day, week after week, but often there's no improvement. Despite the practice, nothing gets better. Until one day you wake up and it is better. It's different. All of a sudden, things have somehow slotted into place. Unknowingly, your sub-conscious mind has been at work and now your muscles perform and respond as you initially hoped they would. The skill has been mastered.

Those who study human evolution see this same incremental process at play, albeit on a longer time-frame. Humanity tends not to evolve smoothly, but instead by quantum leaps. The last 10,000 years or so have seen long periods of relative stability interrupted by short episodes of transformation, usually prompted by sudden advances in technology. As a species we've moved from the world of hunter-gatherers to ever-more complex societies based on agriculture and then science and industry.

For many historians and philosophers, the chaos and uncertainty we currently see around us is evidence of society being in the midst of the next quantum leap. Furthermore, many of these same philosophers and thought-leaders believe that our success in negotiating this leap, in navigating our way through this transition, will depend to a large degree on how we re-design our institutions and organisations, ones which seem increasingly outdated and unable to cope with the complexities we're facing.

In "Reinventing Organisations", Frederic Laloux turns the spotlight onto this changing world of work. He looks to the future, and, interestingly, what he sees might surprise you. Because his vision is a reassuringly optimistic one. As he says at the very start of his book, "There is a reason to be deeply hopeful. The pain we feel is the pain of something old that is dying ... while something new is waiting to be born."

For him, the "something old that is dying" are the assorted organisational models which have become established over past decades and which we still commonly meet:-

- *Dying* – what Laloux calls the "Impulsive" model, the one we see all-too-often in small entrepreneurial organisations, where there is strong Top-down authority, often from an all-powerful Alpha-Male. Such organisations are undoubtedly agile and reactive, but the challenge they face is scalability. How do you take it to the next level? Time and again alpha-male entrepreneurs find control and authority and power hard to relinquish, hard to "let go" of.

- *Dying* – the "Traditional" model, one which relies heavily on bureaucracy, replicable processes and a clear organisation structure. Everyone knows their place in the hierarchy and, provided they do as they're told, they expect a Job-for-life. Such organisations are made for a stable and predictable world, but in our more volatile, uncertain, complex and ambiguous world they can find it hard to adapt.

- *Dying* – the "Achievement" model, the one most widespread in the current corporate world, one which sees the organisation as an efficient machine whose sole aim is to pursue ever-increasing profits. It's a Darwinian "Survival-of-the-fittest" model where people rise up the ladder supposedly based on merit alone. It's a model which claims that anything is possible, anyone can get to the top. Unfortunately, it's also a model based on relentless growth, which, as is now all too evident, is something of a challenge on a finite planet.

- *Dying* – the "Pluralist" model, one where the organisation sees itself as a family or community. Its aim is to create a Values-driven culture where employees feel empowered and look after one another. But making empowerment work on a large scale is a challenge and often there is a disconnect between words and actions, between what is said in the C-Suite and what actually happens at the coal face.

Of course, these are just models, descriptions designed to simplify reality and help us understand and make sense of different organisational behaviours that we encounter – how an organisation recruits, how it manages performance, how it budgets, how it develops a strategy, how it treats its employees. In truth, all organisations are far more complicated than any of these simplistic frameworks would suggest, and they are inevitably a mixture of two or three styles. After all, this is the real world. It's not Crufts dog show. There are no "pure breeds" here. All organisations are mongrels to some degree.

As these models gradually disappear and die – as Laloux believes they will – what other paradigms might emerge and take their place? Of course, it's early days, but Laloux offers, what he calls, an "Evolutionary" worldview as a possible contender. From an individual perspective it's a world that acknowledges our personal craving for both wholeness and connection – connection with our friends and families, our communities, our environment, and also the many sides of ourselves. It's a world where we are drawn to fulfil our unique potential within this connected whole, where we look within and focus on what matters to us (rather than looking outwards and focusing on what matters to others), one where we seek to ask "Am I being true to myself?", "Who am I becoming?", "Is this decision the 'right' decision for me?".

The organisation as a living system

How does this translate into the world of organisations? Well, a metaphor that seems particularly appropriate and relevant to these uncertain times is that of the organisation as a living system. As has just been suggested, the Machine model is far too grey and utilitarian for our modern age. The Family model might seem more colourful and personal, but inevitably comes with built-in assumptions of inequality and authority – Boss = Parent whilst Employee = Child.

A Living System model, on the other hand – think David Attenborough programmes about The Great Barrier Reef – immediately conveys images of self-organisation and wholeness and emergence. In any eco-system there is immeasurable complexity, and yet everything happens just as and when it should and a balance is somehow maintained, all without any need for centralised command processes.

Could this really occur in the world of work? Could an organisation operate as effortlessly and smoothly as a shoal of fish or perhaps even a whole eco-system? Could organisations exist without Managers and without traditional structures? Well, yes, they could. And, yes, they do! There are organisations of every type – for profit and not-for-profit: small SMEs to 10,000+ employees: in every sector, from manufacturing to healthcare, from education to retail, and from energy to IT – organisations that operate using this "Evolutionary" systemic worldview. And in many of these organisations Management has all but been dispensed with. It's not just been reduced as a result of empowering employees. Management has actually been taken out of the equation, in some instances, completely.

In the following essay we'll explore in more detail how this transition might emerge, in particular looking at 3 aspects:

- Self-management
- Wholeness
- Evolutionary purpose

For the moment, however, my questions
for you to reflect on are these:

*Leaving aside the "How" questions for the moment, what might
some of the benefits be to your organisation if you could somehow
dispense with "management"?*

*How does management sometimes hinder the delivery
of your particular client offering?*

How might dispensing with management affect staff morale?

What might the effect on clients be?

The Organisation as a Living System

"A living system continually re-creates itself.
But how this occurs in social systems such as
global institutions depends on our level of
awareness, both individually and collectively.
As long as our thinking is governed by
industrial, "machine age" metaphors such as
control, predictability, and "faster is better",
we will continue to re-create institutions
as we have, despite their increasing
disharmony with the larger world."

Betty Sue Flowers

In the previous essay we looked at a variety of existing organisational models – the Impulsive, the Traditional, the Achievement, and the Pluralist models as Frederic Laloux refers to them – and we saw very briefly how he believes that they are all past their sell-by date. It's not so much that there was anything wrong per se in these individual ways of designing organisational life. They all had some merits, some positive aspects. And they probably still have a certain relevance in a few special situations. But Laloux argues that they are, by and large, inadequate for the volatile, uncertain, complex, and ambiguous world that most organisations now find themselves in. He believes these old models are dying and that the time has come for us to reinvent our organisations. At the same time, he's excited because he feels that ... "something new is waiting to be born". Quite what new structural models might emerge and what they might look like, nobody can be sure. There will doubtless be many contenders. For the time being, though, Laloux has thrown his own hat in the ring and offers what he calls the "Evolutionary" model.

As I suggested in the last essay, this worldview sees the organisation as a living system, one characterised by:

- Self-management
- Wholeness
- Evolutionary purpose

Given that these all fundamentally challenge traditional thinking about Management, I want to explore each in turn.

SELF-MANAGEMENT

For centuries, perhaps millenia, we've organised our institutions as hierarchies, pyramids with an alpha-male – it's usually been a male – at the very top, and everyone else scrambling below to achieve some level of significance. Whether they're Kings, Prime Ministers, Presidents, Popes, Archbishops, Admirals, Generals, Air Marshalls, CEOs, MDs, it seems we love to have someone on top of the pile, someone we can look up to, someone whom we like to pretend is "all knowing and all powerful", someone whom we believe will make the right decisions, someone whom we hope will keep us safe when the going gets tough. And, perhaps most importantly, someone whom we can blame when the whole enterprise goes pear-shaped.

Hierarchies clearly had a role at some point, but do they have a place in our 21st century world? Can they cope in modern times? Is it realistic to expect a few people at the top to be able to handle all the complexities that our institutions now face? I don't wish to be an apologist for politicians – rest assured, I can rail against them as well as the next person – but I do wonder sometimes whether the jobs we give them are now just too difficult for one person. Whatever we might think of Boris Johnson, Theresa May, David Cameron, Gordon Brown or Tony Blair, none of whom covered themselves in glory during their time "at the top", it's fair to say that they're not stupid. And they're all certainly very well educated. And they worked hard. So how did they all come to screw up so badly?

Could it be that they are victims of an outdated hierarchical system which no longer can cope with the world it's trying to manage? I only ask because if everyone "fails" a test, if everyone "gets the wrong answer", might it be time to look at the questions we're asking and see if they're fair and realistic?

We've all experienced the "busy-ness" of corporate life. Well, nowhere is this more visible than at the very top. Leaders in organisations are insanely overworked. There is always an endless stream of decisions that have to be made. There's never enough time, never enough information. But the buck stops with them. So, a decision has to be made. And quickly. There's an assumption that it has to be this way, that if they slow down, if more time is taken, then the organisation will grind to a halt. There's a recognition that the pyramid structure inevitably creates a bottleneck. And so, as soon as one decision is made it's immediately followed by a shout of "Next!". And off they go again.

Pyramid structures just don't work for complex systems. Think of the brain: tens of billions of cells to coordinate, and yet there is no ExCo or SLT to make the final decision. Think of the global economy: millions of companies, billions of customers, trillions of choices made every day, and yet there is no CEO or MD. Think of flocks of starlings: tens of thousands of birds swarming at high speed and close proximity to each other, yet never colliding. It's hard to imagine how hierarchy and central decision-making could ever cope with that amount of complexity.

"Yes, but…"

"…does Self-Management mean that people can do whatever they want, that anything goes?"

No, not at all. Whilst there is no "Boss" there are still structures, people still have defined roles, and there are still clear decision-making processes.

"...does Self-Management mean that we spend all our time in meetings?"

No, not at all. Decision making is actually simpler and more powerful (because the most appropriate person is making the decision), and this results in fewer meetings not more.

"...isn't Self-Management still all very theoretical and experimental?"

No, not at all. There are organisations employing 1000s of people that have thrived for decades using these principles. And they continue to show remarkable resilience.

In all the examples mentioned above – the brain, the global economy, a flock of starlings – rather than a traditional pyramid, what we see instead are structures of distributed authority. In the Evolutionary model that Frederic Laloux is proposing, instead of there being a "Power Hierarchy" with a boss who hires and fires, sets pay levels, and makes the final decisions, what we find is that a host of natural hierarchies spontaneously emerge. It's not about making everyone equal. But it is about allowing all employees to become the best and strongest and healthiest version of themselves. And, as I've just mentioned, it is about decisions being made by the most appropriate people. As Laloux explains: "The goal is not to make everybody equally powerful, but rather to make everyone fully powerful".

WHOLENESS

In my work with teams and individuals, the discussion often turns to how people show up in the workplace compared with how they are at home. The implication is that we're different in these two environments, that we show opposing sides of our personalities to our work colleagues and to our families.

And, to be fair, some people do. A client once described to me how she very consciously negotiated the daily transition from home to work. Each morning, having driven to the office, she would take off her flat-soled driving shoes and replace them with her high-heels. Once she was "suited and booted", she felt she could then face the day, be the person that she needed to be in her role.

Is hers an extreme case? Possibly. But "dressing up", wearing a uniform, is something that many people do. It's common in many workplaces – think the clergy, the military, hospitals, restaurants, shops. As well as showing our level and status within the organisation, a uniform also fundamentally demonstrates that we belong, that we have a role in this place. But at the same time, it also signifies that by belonging to the organisation we no longer fully belong to ourselves. By agreeing to "fit in", to behave in ways that are proper and desirable, we relinquish something of ourselves.

Speaking our truth can be risky, and so we all wear a professional mask, a work persona which enables us to hide the parts of our personalities which we deem to be less acceptable to the powers-that-be. The effect on the organisation of this "personality censorship", however, is that the company gets only a portion, often a small portion, of what it's actually paying for. When staff feel obliged to leave large amounts of their personality "at home" a great deal of potential is wasted. If you're employing staff why wouldn't you want 100% of what they have to offer?

Of course, some employers get it more right than others. There's a young Financial Services organisation in London which, as a place to work, I have often described as being "thrilling". This might seem an odd description, an exaggerated claim. It's certainly a word I have never used about any other company. But in this instance it really does seem to be the right word. And why is it a "thrilling" place? It's all down to the people. And how they're treated. They are valued. There's a belief within the organisation that everyone matters. And, not only that, but diversity matters. They welcome mavericks. They embrace difference. They don't just talk about it or pay lip service to it. As an organisation they believe it and they live it. It doesn't matter what you look like, what you sound like, how you dress, where you come from, what your ethnic background is, what your belief system is, what your academic record is. If you can do your job and you buy into the inspiring vision, then they want you. And, most importantly, they want all of you. 100%. Or as close to that figure as possible. They don't want you to leave large parts of yourself at home. In a very positive way they want you all. The notion is simple: if you're fully there then you will be fully alive. And that means that the organisation will be alive. And that's why I find it thrilling, so much more than other organisations I go and visit. As Frederic Laloux remarks: "If so many workplaces seem lifeless, it is perhaps because we bring so little life to work."

EVOLUTIONARY PURPOSE

In later essays about Change, I will explore in some depth some of the traditional models and compare them with a model from the world of Gestalt therapy. By way of introduction, I want to mention an article written in 1970 by the Gestalt therapist, Arnold Beisser. It was entitled "The Paradoxical Theory of Change", and in it he turned the traditional world of "change" on its head. In contrast to Kurt Lewin's all too prevalent "Unfreeze – Change – Refreeze" model, Beisser's view of working with an individual was …

> "Change occurs when one becomes what he is,
> not when he tries to become what he is not."

Beisser continued: "Change does not take place through a coercive attempt by the individual or by any other person to change him, but it does take place if one takes the time and effort to be what he is – to be fully invested in his current positions. By rejecting the role of change agent, we make meaningful and orderly change possible."

Whilst he was describing individual 1-2-1 therapeutic change, his approach can be applied just as easily to change within an organisation, which after all is simply a collection of individuals.

Beisser's approach is one that suggests "emergence". He uses the word "becomes", in the same way that Robert Chia and Haridimos Tsoukas think we should talk about organisational "becoming", instead of "organisational change". In the same vein, Frederic Laloux advocates we "dance with what wants to emerge" rather than "trying to force the future into existence."

Naturally, these emergent approaches to change don't sit too well with the more directive standard corporate Mission Statement. But then Mission Statements often no longer sit well with employees, who view them as being hollow and redundant and not actually driving decision making.

One company that does take its purpose very seriously is Monzo, the new digital bank. If you go onto their website there is a blog by Tom Blomfield, Monzo's CEO, describing how they arrived at their mission, and how it helps them keep a check on where they're heading, keeps them together, and helps them grow. But most importantly, for Tom it's a reminder of what truly matters. For him Monzo's mission articulates "why we really exist, beyond what we do or how we do it."

A note on strategy – could it be like riding a bike?

Brian Robertson – that's the Brian Robertson who is CEO of Holacracy, not the guitarist from Thin Lizzy – talks of the change in mindset that's needed in modern organisations, a move, as he sees it, from "predict and control" to "sense and respond". He uses the analogy of going on a bike ride, let's say from Land's End to John O' Groats. Now, if a company was in charge of this trip then we all know how it would pan out. First, there would be endless meetings where we'd try and predict the future. We'd decide exactly where we want to be and when, and then we'd try and assess not just every detail of the road ahead, but also where we want and need to be at any particular time. We'd create charts and schedules, and then employ managers to ensure that everything goes according to plan. And when it doesn't go to plan – because of a flat tyre, or an unforeseen diversion, or bad weather, or 101 other unknowns – we would regroup and reassess. We would agree to do things differently next time, to gather more data, to plan more carefully, to refine our goals, to improve our due diligence, to put more controls and measures in place. Because for years we've convinced ourselves that these steps will make a difference.

Does this sound familiar? Of course it does. And yet, we all know that riding a bike is nothing like this. Instead of a "predict and control" mindset, we all ride by using a "sense and respond" mindset, one where we are "in the moment", where, consciously and unconsciously we take in and process vast amounts of data, where we are constantly dealing with an unfolding and ever changing landscape in front of us. And we do it all perfectly. Thousands of micro-adjustments handled seamlessly. Does this approach imply a lack of direction? Does it mean that we are riding aimlessly, going around in circles? Of course not. Our purpose gives us a very clear direction. But the difference is that we are being pulled towards it in an emergent way. The future is flowing freely towards us rather than being "forced into existence". Instead of pushing, we let it happen. And that feels very different.

So, with this clearer image of an organisation as a living system in our minds, my questions for you to reflect on are these:

What do you find most appealing in what you've been reading? What excites you most? In particular what connects deeply with you? What moves you?

If you were going to start a company from scratch, what would be its noble purpose? What purpose would it want to serve? And what form would allow it to best serve that purpose?

*When thinking about how you would like your workplace to be,
what do you desire most? What changes would be most meaningful to you?
Is it in the area of Self-Management, Wholeness or Purpose?*

*When thinking about your own workplace, what do your people desire most?
For which change is there most energy? What's the biggest blockage that is
waiting to be cleared? What energy could be unleashed? What would be the
result of releasing this power? What effect could it have?*

Theme and Variations – Leading

Theme – The Experience of Leadership

"Leadership is not a person or a position.
It is a complex moral relationship between people
based on trust, obligation, commitment, emotion,
and a shared vision of the good."

Joanne Ciulla

Outside of the "day job" my over-riding passion is Music. As a boy I was a chorister and ever since then I have sung in choirs – ranging from the London Symphony Chorus to The Academy of St Martin in the Fields, and currently including Hereford Cathedral. When we talk about Western Classical Music we have, give or take a decade or two, 600 years' worth of repertoire to choose from. There is so much music – in effect, a limitless resource – that newcomers can easily experience a Where-do-I-start type of panic: they want to know more, but are overwhelmed by the enormity of the task.

One potential "way in", of course, is to download and listen to a selection of famous pieces, in the hope that you will gain, presumably via osmosis, an understanding and enthusiasm for the works. From experience, this is a doomed venture, comparable only with attempting to comprehend American Football by watching the Super Bowl without any explanation. After three hours you will be none the wiser, and instead of the hoped-for enlightenment there will simply be bewilderment and confusion.

An alternative strategy is to get some guidance by signing up for a Music Appreciation workshop. When I've run these myself, my opening question – "What are you hoping for?" – tends to elicit fairly standard responses: "I'd like to know what a symphony or a fugue is" … or … "I want to understand more about harmony and rhythm" … or … "I want to know more about the history of music."

As a result, it's tempting to design programmes in a very reductionist way: to look at, say, Form – Symphonies, Sonatas, Oratorios, Motets, Passions, Variations, Preludes, Toccatas, Fugues, and so on – and study what they are, and why and when composers choose to use them. Another strategy is to focus instead on the mechanics of music – Tempo, Rhythm, Harmony, Melody – and explore how a composer uses these "building blocks" to create such a towering structure as a symphony. Yet another method would be to examine music through the lens of history, exploring the lives of the great composers – Bach, Mozart, Beethoven, Brahms et al – discovering where they sat in the various "periods" – Renaissance, Baroque, Classical, Romantic, Modern, Post-modern.

All of these approaches can tell us a great deal about the music. But, at the same time they run the risk of killing the very thing they're studying. A piece of music is a live, breathing, work of recreation, that is so much more than the sum of its parts. Yes, a knowledge of the work's historical context, and an understanding of how to analyse a piece harmonically can add greatly to our enjoyment. But we must always remember that these features are not the music! They are not what we experience when we listen.

It's akin to dissecting animals in the biology lab; unfortunately, something dies in the process. Studying the anatomy of, say, a frog, how its component parts fit together, how its varied processes – brain function, blood circulation, digestion, respiration, reproduction – all work together as a single system, can be very interesting and helpful. Helpful, that is, to everyone except the frog. The one missing element in these various analyses – the most important element – is that we experience a frog as a single entity, as a living, breathing creature, not as a collection of anatomical parts or processes. Certainly, it can add to our appreciation and wonder of a frog to be able to distinguish previously unknown details, but these can never be a substitute for the "whole", for the "experience".

The same, I would argue, applies to the discipline of Leadership. If you're a student of Leadership there's really no shortage of material out there for you to get your teeth into. On Amazon – just in the Books section – there's an endless array of memoirs and stories and perspectives and theories and models: whatever your taste, there's something for everyone. But here's the rub: that very diversity leads to confusion because there's almost no agreement amongst the authors. And not just about details but about the big things, the very nature of the subject, even the definition of the word. Take ten titles at random and you'll find ten different definitions of the word Leadership. Indeed, choose a hundred titles, or a thousand and I suspect the result will be the same. There are as many definitions as there are writers.

Despite this profusion of views it's still tempting to believe that finding a single, all-encompassing definition is both desirable and possible; surely we could get authors and academics and business leaders to agree at least on what we're talking about. Can it really be that difficult? Surely we just need to start again, be clearer and more precise with our terms of reference, and try harder.

But what if we look at the situation another way? What if we start with the evidence gleaned from thousands of writers and scholars – that instead of there being one single meaning there are actually multiple definitions of the word Leadership? What might this tell us? Could it be suggesting, for example, that Leadership is not some entity that we can isolate and examine objectively under a metaphorical microscope, but is instead something we experience subjectively; that Leadership is relational, that every Leadership experience is individual, that every example of Leadership is inherently unique and personal, and so needs to be examined holistically?

The Leadership Moment

In her hugely refreshing book, Rethinking Leadership, Prof. Donna Ladkin introduces what she calls The Leadership Moment. For her, this Leadership Moment describes the inter-dependence of four separate and distinct components of Leadership all of which have to be in existence for "Leadership" to be experienced. (Just to be clear, she uses the term "moment" in its philosophical sense rather than referring to a moment-in-time).

These four components, all essential for a complete Leadership experience, are:

- The Leader
- The Follower
- The Task
- The Context

Whilst this might at first appear to be yet another Four Quadrant model, or 2x2 Matrix, there is a subtle but essential difference. It is a holistic model; as just mentioned, all four of these components have to be present for Leadership to be experienced. You can't leave any of them out. Yes, you can examine these components individually, but you can never study them in isolation. They must always be explored in relation to each other.

If we create a visual model it might make the idea clearer. Take the triangular-based pyramid shown here: there are four separate faces to this pyramid (including the base). And we can describe any one of these four separate faces individually. But at all times we must be aware that without any one of them the structure is no longer "a pyramid". The faces must be described in relation to the whole – to "the moment".

The traditional method of examining Leadership – of breaking it down into some agreed number of components and then measuring them using psychometric tools – is a particularly reductionist approach. Its neatness and simplicity can be very appealing – the so-called "seduction of reduction" – but there's an ever-present danger of falling into the trap of examining topics in isolation. (I am, of course, more than aware that this could happen in these "Reflections", and so all I can urge you to do is to keep part of your attention on "the whole", while we bring some focus to each Reflection in turn.)

The dangers of slipping inadvertently into a more certain and inflexible style – along the lines of "The 10 Secrets of Effective Leadership!" – is that such an approach is incapable of describing the full experience of Leadership and can only ever hint at how it has been lived through by those involved. In the same way that dissecting a frog tells us everything about the frog except what it's like to be a frog or experience a frog, Donna Ladkin describes reductionist approaches as "collapsing" Leadership, as if the fullness of the experience has been removed to leave but a shadow. It's rather like the following image. "On the ground" we see some simple circles, but those same circles could result from a sphere, or a cylinder or a cone. If we "collapse" these three-dimensional shapes to two-dimensions we lose so much – in fact everything that is important. Likewise, when we "collapse" Leadership to a trite list of qualities we run the risk of doing the same.

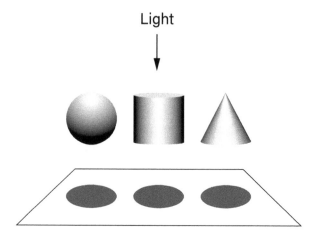

So, my questions for you to reflect on are these:

How would you define Leadership? How does your definition describe the fullness of the experience?

From your own experience choose an example of good Leadership. Why do you remember it so positively? Why was it so effective? How would its effectiveness have been different if the Context or the Task had been different?

Think of a time when you experienced Leadership differently from one of your colleagues. Why did it work/not work for you and for them?

Variation 1 – Why have people given you permission to lead?

"Leadership is much less about what you do, and much more about who you are. If you view leadership as a bag of manipulative tricks or charismatic behaviours to advance your own personal interest, then people have every right to be cynical. But if your leadership flows first and foremost from inner character and integrity of ambition, then you can justly ask people to lend themselves to your organisation and its mission."

Frances Hesselbein

As we've just seen, Donna Ladkin's Leadership Moment describes the inter-dependence of four separate and distinct components of Leadership:

- The Leader
- The Follower
- The Context
- The Task

In each experience of Leadership we always need to consider not just you, the leader – your personality, gifts, skills, and experience – but also those whom you're leading, the followers. As the saying goes "Different folks need different strokes". The way a conductor might lead an inexperienced Student orchestra will not be effective with or indeed tolerated by a world-class group such as The London Symphony. Likewise, the approaches you use to lead a cohort of new graduates have to be different from those you use with your senior colleagues.

When it comes to "Followers" it's also interesting to consider the notion of "permission", that if Leaders want to take action it is only possible if the followers allow them. This certainly can occur in the orchestral world. You go to a concert at the Royal Albert Hall where the XYZ Philharmonic is being conducted by Maestro Q. All looks OK to the audience. But what you don't realise is that the orchestra has long since lost confidence in Maestro Q and doesn't rate him. So what actually is happening is that the players are ignoring him, letting him dance in front of them for an hour-and-a-half, and they are all taking their cues from the Concert Master/First Violinist.

Is this exclusively a Concert Hall problem? Of course not. It happens in organisations all the time – a team loses confidence in their boss and so they just ignore them and go their own way. In effect, they take away that "permission" that the boss once had to lead them. It's worth remembering that in any group situation, we give permission to certain people to lead us, and we withhold it or remove it from others. Rob Goffee and Gareth Jones have written tellingly about this in "Why Should Anyone Be Led By You?"

This brings us to the task. One reason that your followers might take back or withhold their permission is that you're using an inappropriate approach, one that worked perhaps for Task A but doesn't work for the current Task B. If an orchestra is tackling a brand new and very difficult large-scale piece then the players would probably welcome extremely precise directions. But if you use the same micro-management approach when conducting Mozart then you'll just get in their way and they'll start doing their own thing. In organisations it's just the same. Does a directive approach designed for Emergencies (a burning house, a sinking ship) translate well to the everyday workplace, where things are by definition more stable? Is a highly regimented system that works well in, say, an Army unit in Afghanistan really suitable for a residential Hospice in Woking, or an entrepreneurial Hi-Tech start-up in Silicon Valley? Naturally, when we look at extreme cases such as these we can all pat ourselves on the back and say "I would never do anything so crass". But what if the positions are not so extreme? Are you really as flexible in your approach as you think?

And then, finally, within this Leadership Moment there's the context. Where, in time, is this leadership experience taking place? What came before? What is it following? The world of politics gives us countless examples that illustrate this point neatly: Winston Churchill in 1940 (early on in WW2), John F Kennedy in 1960 (the continuing Cold War), Margaret Thatcher in 1979 (following the "Winter of Discontent"), Tony Blair in 1997 (following 18 years of "Tory sleaze"), New York Mayor, Rudy Giuliani, in 2001 (after 9/11), Barack Obama in 2009 (following 8 years of George W. Bush). Leaders are invariably "of their time", and it's impossible to transfer one set of behaviours to another situation. These six politicians all had undoubted qualities which served them well when those virtues were needed. But, for three of them – Churchill, Thatcher and Blair – those very same qualities were of little use when the times changed. And the result was that they were ignominiously removed from office.

Everything appears different depending on what it's surrounded by, and it can never be divorced from that context. For example, take you as an individual, the many guises you have and the way you appear differently to different people. Think of all the groups – work, social, family – that you're a part of, and then take a moment to think of how you're seen in each one, how you behave in each one. The differences can be intriguing: "Why is it I can show this part of my personality to Group A, but not to Group B?" ... "Why does Group C view me this way whereas Group D sees the opposite?

Context is key. For instance, take a look at the image opposite. It's a simple picture of two vertical bars of different shades of grey set against a background of some horizontal black and white stripes. No problems so far.

The two vertical bars, A and B, appear to be different – A, the one on the left is obviously a lighter grey and, B, the one on the right is darker. But they're not. The two bars are the same colour. EXACTLY the same colour.

I know they don't look it, and I know you're thinking "No, they're not". But Yes they are! The wavelength of the light entering your eyes from the two grey bars is precisely the same. Of course, the two colours don't LOOK the same, but that's because the business of "seeing" and making sense of the world around us involves so much more than just reacting to the light entering your eyes. When we "see", all manner of processing is going on in the brain to make allowances for other factors such as the surroundings. That's one reason that we all see things so differently.

A   B

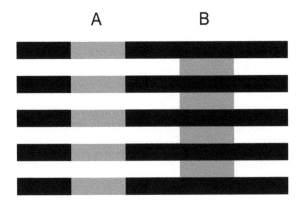

Everything is an interpretation. Although we're brought up to think that we always see things "as they are", that's just wishful thinking. The truth is that, unless we've had specialist training (for example, as an artist) we invariably will see things "as we THINK they are". It's worth bearing this in mind next time you think about the strengths and weaknesses of one of your colleagues. Or, indeed, if you're ever tempted to ask "Which is the 'real' me?" Who you are, the person you are, the leader you are, all depends on the context. And the stories you tell yourself.

So, my questions for you to reflect on are these:

Why have your colleagues given you permission to lead them? What particular qualities do they see in you? Why are those qualities so relevant at the moment?

If they – the followers – were different, would you still be the best person to lead? If so, Why? If not, Why not?

If the context – the time and place – were different, would you still be the best person to lead? If so, Why? If not, Why not?

If the task – the job which needs to be done or the problem that needs to be solved – were different, would you still be the best person to lead? If so, Why? If not, Why not?

How might things change in the future? What might cause your colleagues to take back that "permission to lead"?

Think of a time when, as a leader, you used an approach which was inappropriate; an approach that might have worked with Team X but not with your Team Y. What could you have done differently?

Think of some work teams that you are part of, ones where you show contrasting sides of your personality. Why do you behave differently in these situations? How might each team benefit from seeing and experiencing "more of you"?

Variation 2 –
The Elusiveness of Leadership

"Leadership is like beauty - it's hard to define but
you know it when you see it."

Warren G. Bennis

Leadership is hard to study. We've already seen that it is difficult to define – there are as many definitions as there are researchers – and this has led some to conclude that the subject is an academic dead-end, no longer worthy of attention. Others go further still, claiming that the lack of an adequate definition brings the very existence of leadership as a concept into question. There are academics who ask "Is leadership even real?"

Whilst I accept and acknowledge the definitional difficulties, and even though I struggle to get to grips with it, I remain intrigued by the idea of Leadership. Like Love, it is one of those things that "we all know it when we experience it", we all "know what we mean" by it, and yet at the same time it is surprisingly 'slippery' as a concept. It's hard to pin down. But why might that be?

Perhaps the first problem is that it's intangible. As we've seen, leadership is not so much a "thing" which can be dissected, but is instead an aspect of a living relationship. When we discussed Donna Ladkin's "Leadership Moment" we saw that there were four elements, all of which must be present – the Leader, the Follower, the Task and the Context. This suggests that Leadership is relational, that it exists in some form of "betweenness", in the inner world of those who experience it, a hidden space which obviously is not easily accessible to others.

And then there's the idea that leadership is hard to locate because it's always on the move. Leadership doesn't reside simply with the "leader". It is not "static" but instead moves around the group. Back in the 1950s and 1960s the Australian psychologist, Cecil Gibb, differentiated two qualities that he called "headship" and "leadership". Headship, he said, is a "positional authority" and lies with the person who enjoys hierarchical power, the one who is nominally "in-charge" – the Team leader, the Director, the CEO, the MD. By definition "headship" is fairly static. Those individuals who have positional power tend to keep it for significant periods of time. By contrast, Gibb saw "leadership" as something different, "a process of influence", one that sits with whichever person in the group is currently being most influential. This idea was embodied thirty years later by the English Rugby coach, Sir Clive Woodward. For him, regardless of who's wearing the captain's armband (and therefore has "headship") the leadership lies with the player with the ball. For those few moments that player is leading and therefore decides the direction of play. Seconds later yet another player is leading, and so it goes on. The leadership is forever moving around. It changes from moment to moment and also in ways that are hard to predict. This makes it tricky to spot. After all, where should you look?

A further problem with trying to isolate leadership is one identified by Peter Gronn, another Australian leadership researcher. He proposed that leadership can't be seen in and of itself, but can only be identified by its consequences – much in the way that we can rarely see the wind but instead have to rely on looking for its effects. But what if these effects are not instant but take time to appear? If we accept leadership as being "a process of influence", that influence may take a long time to come to fruition. Think of some of the people – inspirational teachers, perhaps – who influenced you as a child. The effect they had on you may have taken years, perhaps decades, to mature. All those years ago there was probably little to observe, few overt signs of leadership, though it was clearly there in some form.

And then, finally, I want to mention the philosopher, Martin Heidegger, and, in particular, two of his concepts – "ready-to-hand" and "present-at-hand". To explain these ideas simply, let's take an everyday scenario such as going to the shops in the car. You open the car door, you settle yourself inside, you switch on the engine, you put on your seat-belt, you select the right gear, you release the handbrake, you depress the accelerator and off you go. No problem at all: everything happens smoothly. The point is though that you probably thought of none of these individual pieces of equipment – the car key, the door handle, the clutch, the gear stick, the accelerator, the hand-brake – you thought of none of them during the process of starting off and driving to the shops. Every part of the car worked correctly – it was "ready-to-hand" – and you engaged with it in an unconscious way. And that's how we all tend to operate. That is, until something goes wrong, until something fails and we get the experience of turning the key in the ignition and nothing happening. Immediately we behave differently. We now notice and are aware of the engine precisely because it is NOT working. Rather than being on auto-pilot, we step back and examine every aspect for what could have gone wrong, what's failed, what's broken, what's changed, what's missing. Rather than simply using the car we now interact with it as it presents itself to us; we move from "ready-to-hand" to "present-at-hand".

And it's not just the car in this scenario. There is you. But how often do you think of "you", of your body? When things are OK and you're reasonably fit and healthy, probably not much at all. But if you wake up with a stiff neck, and you try to get into the car then suddenly your body is the focus of your attention. Once again, you're aware of it precisely because it's not working properly.

An important feature of these two ways of interacting is that when we engage with something in a "ready-to-hand" way, that "something" disappears. Think about your drive to the shops: not only can you probably not remember most of the journey – the various twists and turns of the road – but you are probably also unaware of the car, simply because it's doing what it should. When things work they frequently become invisible, and are only noticeable by their failure or absence. In exactly the same way that the car can become "invisible" when all is well, when a team of people is thriving and performing as they should, the leadership can be hard to spot. Things "just happen". Ironically, leadership moves to the forefront and we become conscious of it often at the very moment that it becomes absent.

So, my questions for you to reflect on are these:

When have you experienced a team where things "just happened"? What were you all involved in? How did things "just happen"?

What form did the leadership take? Where was it? How visible was it?

When have you experienced the difference between "headship" and "leadership"? Did the person with "headship" actively encourage the idea of "leadership"?

When you think of people that influenced you as a child, what form did it take? How long did it take for that influence to come to fruition?

What would their "leadership" have looked like all those years ago? How obvious was it?

When have you been made aware of leadership by its very absence? What was happening? What was not happening? What was missing?

Variation 3 – Passing the baton

"I love to hear a choir.
I love the humanity ... to see the faces of real people
devoting themselves to a piece of music.
I like the teamwork. It makes me feel optimistic
about the human race when I see them
cooperating like that."

Paul McCartney

When is the Leader in charge?

In the previous essay we came across the Australian psychologist, Cecil Gibb, and the distinction he made between what he called "Headship" and "Leadership". In this essay I want to explore this idea in some more depth.

Some years ago I was singing for the first time in St Paul's Cathedral in London. For a multitude of reasons St Paul's is special – its size, its beauty, its acoustic, its history. It's a wonderful place to visit and walk around, and every year more than one million tourists do exactly that. But at the end of the day these visitors are merely bystanders, onlookers, never quite experiencing the building as it was envisaged in the 1660s by Christopher Wren. On the other hand, to be able to sing services or perform in a building like St Paul's, to be an active "participant" in its musical life, to sing your heart out in such a place is something else. It's a thrilling experience. And an opportunity not given to many.

As often happens during rehearsals in cathedrals, there were quite a few tourists listening. As we finished our run through I remember thinking "If I was to go and ask any of those people in the nave 'Who was leading this?' I bet they'd all reply 'The conductor, obviously.

He's the one in charge. He's the one at the front. He must be the one who is leading'." But, for me as a performer, I know that it's far more complicated than this. The conductor may well be leading. But not always, not all the time. There's a lot more going on.

When I say that the conductor isn't always "leading" I'm not being critical in the slightest. At St Paul's there were plenty of times during the evening concert when he was, when all of our eyes were on him. But then there were at least as many moments when the leadership was NOT with him. Instead, it was with some of us. As we saw in the previous essay, as Cecil Gibb would have described it, whilst the conductor has "headship", he doesn't always have "leadership".

The work we were singing that particular day opens gently. But soon the mood becomes more energised with a lively fugue in which the opening statement is given to the basses. Now, of course we've rehearsed it plenty of times, and the conductor has indicated the speed he wants, how he likes it phrased and articulated, and the type of sound he wants. But in the concert, in that moment, whatever has been discussed in the past doesn't much matter. It's about 'Now', and it's up to us to "step forward" (only metaphorically!) and take the lead. The "baton of leadership", if you like, has been given to the basses, and the way we sing this theme will affect how the piece unfolds over the next few pages.

But the leadership doesn't stay with us for long, because as soon as we've stated the fugue subject it's taken up and repeated by the altos. It's now they who are in the driving seat, they who are leading, and we take on a quieter accompanying role. That continues for a couple more lines until the tenors join the fray, and once again, the focus of leadership swings. Soon the sopranos are involved and from then on until the end of the piece the Leadership ping-pongs around the choir. Like the very best of conversations, each voice-part briefly takes the initiative – sometimes just for a couple of bars at a time – and then quietly slips back into the texture while another voice-part comes to the fore. And finally, as the tension builds and the climax of the piece approaches, there's an awareness that someone – or is it "something" – else is doing the leading. Now it's neither the basses nor the sopranos nor any other singer who's leading. It might not even be the conductor. During the closing pages – the climax of the work – it's as if it's the composer who's leading. It's as if Bach himself is driving the performance to its inevitable conclusion. Or maybe it's the work itself, the "task in hand", that's doing the pulling? The end point, the final bar-line, is drawing us all inexorably towards it. Achieving the task as perfectly as possible has become the motivation of all concerned.

In the musical world we are in some ways very fortunate in that we have a clear goal and task to achieve. And we all know what it is: it's to make the score – those inert, lifeless, two-dimensional, notes and marks on the page – come alive in a fully three-dimensional way. You might argue that tasks in the organisational world are less defined and clear-cut, possibly less inspirational. But if that's true, could it be part of the Leader's role – ie: your role – to make your team's objectives more precise and defined and even inspiring. Perhaps then the goal would do all the pulling rather than you, the leader, doing all the pushing.

So, my questions for you to reflect on are these:

When have you seen Clive Woodward's idea – "the leader is the person with the ball" – in action within your team? What was happening? Who was involved? Where did the leadership go next? How did you see your role?

What can you do to ensure that each of your colleagues participates fully in the leadership of your team?

How can you make your goals come alive and become tangible and "three dimensional"?

How can you redefine your team goals so that they are as inspiring to your colleagues as Beethoven and Bach are to a musician? … so that the goals do the pulling rather than you doing the pushing?

Variation 4 –
The Expectations of Leadership

"Before you are a leader, success is all about growing yourself. When you become a leader, success is all about growing others."

Jack Welch

Having lived for 25 years in suburban London, I am now settled in the countryside, out amongst the sheep and cows on the Welsh border in rural Herefordshire. 15 miles north, the county town of Hereford is known for a number of things: its gothic Cathedral (where I sing regularly); the "Mappa Mundi", the oldest map of the world; and being the home of the Special Air Service, better known as the SAS, which has been based in the city since 1960.

Whilst I have no background in the military, I do have an interest in the SAS, in that for a while I was an Associate Course Director at The Leadership Trust, a training organisation based just outside Ross-on-Wye. The Leadership Trust was founded in the 1970s by David Gilbert-Smith who had previously served in the SAS. When he left the service, he decided to adapt and transfer some of the relevant knowledge that he had gained from his time there, and take it with him into industry and commerce.

The stereotypical view of the conventional army is of a near-vertical hierarchy where your seniors are never questioned. When they say "Jump!" you jump, when they say "Now!", you do it NOW! When Gilbert-Smith moved from that conventional army to the SAS, he was immediately struck by the different culture. Instead of a vertical hierarchy, in the SAS he found an almost horizontal hierarchy of command, one which encourages open communication, honesty and directness. The SAS is not looking for sameness and uniformity, but rather promotes being unconventional and original. It wants mature, intelligent soldiers who do their own thinking and take responsibility for their own decisions. Self-control is paramount, and this comes from self-discipline, self-respect and the best use of one's brain, especially when under pressure.

From its inception, the aim of The Leadership Trust has been to make available to the commercial world some of the key concepts from the Special Forces. It provides a range of courses, but its flagship programme has always been the one entitled "Leadership in Management", a week-long residential course where attendees don't just learn the theory of leadership, but truly experience it and are immersed in it. As the week progresses delegates, in multiple groups of 8, are presented with a series of team tasks that become steadily more difficult, lengthy and complex. Task 1 on Day 1, for example, might be something brief and straightforward to comprehend, one where the team leader simply has to get their team (plus an assortment of barrels, planks and ropes) from point A to point B without touching the ground. Later in the week, however, delegates will be dealing with complex projects lasting 12 hours or more and having to collaborate with various other groups.

The whole programme runs to a precise schedule: there are clocks everywhere, all of which are synchronised. At the start of each task, instructions – on yellow laminate sheets – are handed to a member of the group who has been selected by the facilitators to be the leader for this particular session. Everything the leader needs to know – the nature of the task, the resources available, the roles for individuals, the locations involved, the timings – everything is on the sheets. No questions will be answered. At the start of the week, when the tasks are simple, the instructions are clear and unambiguous and barely fill a side of A4. Later on in the week, however, as the complexity is ramped up, the instructions fill pages. The information you have to sort through is overwhelming. Naturally, some of this information is crucial to completing the task successfully, but these essential nuggets are hidden amongst a stream of irrelevancies and red herrings that somehow have to be assessed and dismissed, all while the clock is ticking.

A central theme of SAS training is "Can you control your mind?" – can you make decisions under pressure, can you avoid panic, can you think clearly when you are exhausted, when you're overwhelmed, when you're frightened? As a result, the Leadership in Management programme ensures that pressure builds inexorably as the week progresses. This is done in a number of ways: firstly, by getting delegates steadily more tired, secondly by making them experience real fear from time to time, and thirdly by making them increasingly overwhelmed and confused. Tiredness is guaranteed because, apart from meals, there is almost no time off. There are no leisurely evenings spent chatting in the bar: the course is purposely full-on. The experience of being frightened is achieved through certain physical activities – climbing, abseiling, caving – designed to help delegates face their fears, experience being "at their limits". And, finally, the sense of being overwhelmed results from the sheer complexity of the final tasks. These have been designed to stretch everyone. So delegates will almost certainly feel out of their depth, unsure of what to do or how to move forward.

So, why has the Leadership Trust designed the programme this way? Why do they focus on discomfort? Why do they build in fear, exhaustion, overwhelm? The answer is simple. They are aiming to replicate the world of work that many of us experience. Almost all of the tasks are "Workplace scenarios" and present challenges that people have to face and deal with every day. Everyone at some point has to perform at work even though they're worn out, even though they're scared, even though they're overwhelmed. The point is always: Can you continue to make sound decisions when everything is conspiring against you? That's the point of the programme.

It's important to emphasise that a key component – perhaps the key component – of the programme is the Post-Task Debrief. As soon as each task finishes delegates are instructed by their facilitator to return to their team meeting room. In preparation for the debrief they walk back in silence. No chatter is allowed. People are alone with their thoughts. Once back in the room, the facilitator starts the debrief by asking each delegate in turn how they are currently feeling. For many this in itself is a challenge, to replace "I think …" with "I am feeling…". But for David Gilbert-Smith it was essential that we be aware of our feelings. Leadership, for him, was about "winning the hearts and minds" of people. (NB: "Hearts" comes first. Emotions THEN intellect.). Yes, we must be able to control our emotions, but first we have to be fully aware of them.

Towards the end of each debrief – which can last up to two hours – the group agree on one or two learnings that they will add to a running list of "Things we'll do next time", behaviours which were absent during this task but need to be present. Frequent suggestions include obvious ones such as "Make sure everyone is involved at all times" … "Listen to everyone's ideas" … "Read the instructions fully before starting the exercise". But an unexpected one that often comes up is "Don't adopt roles". As I've mentioned, as the week progresses the tasks get more complex. But they also, as I've just explained, become more "real", having been designed to simulate "workplace scenarios". In introducing the upcoming challenge the instructions might say things like "You are the CEO of ABC Industries….". There might be a second set of instructions for a group member stating "You are the Group Chairman of ABC Industries…", and perhaps a third set of instructions stating "You are the Group CFO". As the various members read their "yellow laminates" something interesting happens almost every time. The delegates start to play the role that they've been ascribed. This might sound quite positive, but in fact it's just the opposite. More often than not, Delegate #1 is suddenly overwhelmed by thoughts of "I'm supposed to be a CEO. But I've never been a CEO. What would a CEO do? What would a CEO say? How would a CEO act? ….etc….etc…." Meanwhile, Delegate #2 is thinking "I'm supposed to be the Group Chairman. But I've never been a Chairman. What would a Chairman do?". And Delegate #3 is thinking "I'm supposed to be the CFO….etc….

etc....". Almost invariably, the delegates slip into "acting a role", all the time forgetting that the exercise is not about second-guessing what a CEO or Chairman or CFO would do, but it's about realising that this is a TEAM exercise. There are 8 people sitting around the table all of whom have got ideas and could contribute towards accomplishing the task. If everyone could just ignore what's written on the instruction sheets – "I'm a CEO" – and instead put their heads together and work collaboratively, work as a team, to solve a problem, then there would be a far greater chance of success.

But it rarely happens. And even when in the Post-Task Debrief the group agrees that in future they will work as a team and NOT assume roles, guess what happens when the next task begins. As soon as the clock starts ticking and they're under pressure, they immediately start acting out roles.

So, my questions for you to reflect on are these:

When you've taken on new leadership positions, what have been your expectations of yourself? What do you tell yourself about what leaders do and how they act and behave? What effect might these personal expectations have had on your team?

As a new leader, when have you "played a role" and found yourself wondering "What would a CEO / Chairman / CFO / Manager do in this case?"

At some level, as a "leader" have you ever thought that you must know all the answers to any question someone could pose to you? And, inevitably, when you haven't known the answer have you ever felt vulnerable or exposed? Or even a failure?

As a leader, when have you found yourself taking on too much and trying to do it all by yourself? Why is that?

Could you have involved others and collaborated more? Why didn't you? What stopped you? What would that collaboration have looked like? What would the benefits have been for you and your team?

What does "Winning the Hearts and Minds of others" mean to you? As a leader, when have you "Won the Hearts and Minds of others"? How do you know? What happened? What was the effect?

And when have you NOT "Won the Hearts and Minds of others"? What happened? What was the effect? What could you have done differently?

With your team, what is your equivalent of a "Post-Task Debrief? How structured and detailed is it? How do you capture the learnings? What benefits might come from asking your team colleagues "How are you feeling about the task / project / assignment / meeting / plan?"

Variation 5 –
How do you Lead experts?

> "I was never the smartest guy in the room.
> From the first person I hired, I was never the
> smartest guy in the room. And that's a big deal.
> If you're a leader and you're the smartest guy in the
> room, you've got real problems."
>
> *Jack Welch*

People are often promoted to more senior positions as a result of their expertise – the best sales person becomes manager, the best nurse becomes Ward sister, and so on. When that happens to you, you automatically have a certain authority over your colleagues based on your "Been there, Done that" track record.

But what happens if you're not the most technically accomplished person in the group? What do you do then? What is your role as a Leader when every one of those in front of you is truly outstanding, a master of their craft, a better practitioner than you will ever be? What if you're a General Counsel hoping to lead a team of lawyers, all of whom have a greater grasp of the technical details than you do? Or if you're a middle-aged IT Manager leading a group of young programming whizz-kids? What particular challenges does that create?

A few years ago, in their book "Clever" Rob Goffee and Gareth Jones explored this very subject – the challenges of leading smart people, employees who contribute vigorously to an organisation and have an ability to punch far above their weight. I would suggest that professional musicians fall fairly and squarely into this "Clever" category. If you fancy a management challenge then in many ways musicians are it. But, at the same time, they are also a source of potential learning.

Conductors quickly come to terms with just how unbelievably accomplished the players sitting in front of them are. Partly due to "market forces" professional orchestral players are the best of the best. Compared with the number of people employed in, say, Construction or Oil & Gas or Pharma companies, there are really not many performing musicians. And so those that you see on stage in major cities such as London or Birmingham or Chicago or New York are among the very best players around. They're world class. They are all masters of their craft. And so, as a conductor, even though you can probably play an instrument pretty well yourself, you are faced with a situation where each of the 75 players in front of you is without doubt a better instrumentalist than you will ever be. There is NOTHING that you can tell them about playing the violin or the cello or the flute or whatever it is. They are complete experts.

And they've been expert for a long time, from a very young age. Musicians start early. Whilst brass and woodwind players may typically commence their studies in their early teens or just before, professional string players will have begun playing much earlier, probably aged about six. This means that by the time they're eighteen – ie: the age when those in other professions are just beginning their studies at college or university – professional musicians already have a fully developed technique coupled with years of experience of high-level ensemble playing. If you ever want a taste of just how accomplished a group of teenagers can become I urge you to go to a concert by the National Youth Orchestra of Great Britain. Their abilities will astonish you.

But that's not all. If the technical proficiency of orchestral players, the way they get around their instruments, doesn't intimidate you then possibly their musical knowledge and experience will. I remember once chatting with an orchestral string player about his 35-year career, three-and-a-half decades during which he'd played with the Academy of St Martin in the Fields, two other London symphony orchestras, and the orchestra at The Royal Opera House, Covent Garden. As we talked, it eventually became clear that apart from a Tone-poem by Richard Strauss he couldn't think of a single piece of standard repertoire that he hadn't played at some point in his life. Whether it was the big symphonic repertoire, smaller chamber orchestra pieces, operas, or contemporary works written last week, he claimed to have played everything. And most of it multiple times. Perhaps he was exaggerating slightly, but I don't think very much. He and his colleagues simply know a lot. If you're the conductor you have to recognise that players like this know the broad musical landscape at least as well as you do, and in many ways they know it better; they've rehearsed these works and performed them on countless occasions over the past decades, probably every year since they were teenagers. They know their part inside-out, they have strong ideas about how they think the piece should go, and they have very clear memories of past performances, when they were conducted by the greatest conductors of recent decades.

But if these 75 masters-of-their-craft weren't threatening enough individually – especially when you know that each one of them is comparing you unfavourably to conductors that they admire – the real miracle is how they bring it all together and collaborate. The teamwork of any professional orchestra is so staggeringly good that it's really not immediately obvious what help the players need from any outsider like you. Indeed, there are several orchestras around the world who don't need help, who regularly choose to perform by themselves, without a conductor. And whilst these are, admittedly, smaller Chamber ensembles with just 40 or so players, the 75+ players in a large Symphony orchestra can get by extraordinarily well without any obvious external guidance. Admittedly, the London Symphony Orchestra would never perform a piece without a conductor, but they could make a damn good fist of it in rehearsal if they wanted to. Ask them to play a work from the standard repertoire, like a Beethoven Symphony for example, and you'd soon realise that they can cope perfectly well without you. To be honest, you could go and sit down in the auditorium or walk out of the room and the orchestra would carry on quite happily by themselves. And it's not as if the playing would be lifeless or mechanical. Far from it. It would be musical and shaped and expressive: the players would get louder and quieter when they're supposed to, it would be beautifully phrased and accented, they would accelerate and ease up as appropriate, and finally they'd all finish together. And that could continue, if needs be, for all four movements, for the whole 40 minutes of the piece. Perhaps the final ounce of polish may be missing, there may be a few slightly ragged moments, and overall it would probably not be up to "performance standard", but it would be surprisingly good. So much so that I suspect that quite a few concert-goers would be hard pressed to tell the difference between "WITH conductor" and "WITHOUT".

So, my questions for you to reflect on are simple:

As a leader, what would happen if you "sat down in the auditorium"? Would your team be able to carry on without you? Indeed, should they be able to carry on without you?

Is part of your role, perhaps, to develop your team and eventually make yourself redundant? How can you make your team self-sufficient, self-managing? What would be the benefits?

Do any members of your team know the "organisational landscape" even better than you? How can you ensure that this is a +ve and not a –ve?

How do YOU lead people when THEY are the experts and know more than you do, and when they are technically more accomplished that you are? Where do you get your authority from?

Precisely, how do you add value to the various teams you're a member of? And how do you SHOW you add value?

Variation 6 –
Who is your Role model?

"Good evening, ladies and gentlemen.
Can we start with Act 1, Number 3, please."

The occasion for these brief instructions was a London church one night back in October 1994, and they came immediately after a coffee break midway through a choir rehearsal. A group I then sang with had been preparing for a week or two for a forthcoming concert-performance at the Queen Elizabeth Hall of Weber's "Euryanthe". It's an opera that first saw the light of day back in the 1820's but has been rather neglected since – only the orchestral Overture has entered the standard repertoire. This QEH concert was going to be a rare public performance of the whole work.

As a chorus we'd already had a few "note-bashing" rehearsals, and during these we'd reached the conclusion that it was no surprise that "Euryanthe" had been neglected for 150+ years. It seemed second-rate at best, and really not worth the effort of resurrection. To be fair, our chorus master had done a decent job in helping us learn the notes, but after an early "highpoint" our singing quickly went downhill. We didn't care for the piece, we thought it was a waste of our time, and as a result we weren't fully engaged. And so, as the hours slipped by, the more we sang the worse we got. The culmination of this was the first half of this particular rehearsal in question: we were sloppy and lacklustre and making mistakes all over the place.

But then Mark Elder – now Sir Mark Elder – arrived. He was the one who was going to conduct the actual concert the following week and he was there to take the second half of our rehearsal, the first time that Conductor and Chorus had met. And thus it was that he issued the simple instructions: "Good evening, ladies and gentlemen. Can we start with Act 1, Number 3, please."

Simple instructions, yes. But at the same time, somehow electrifying. Suddenly, his eyes were on fire and his whole body was communicating to us that this piece of Weber was not only worth doing, but that there was nothing else more important, that there was nowhere else we should be and nothing else we could possibly have been doing on this damp and cold October evening. It was immediately clear that "Euryanthe" mattered to him. He was totally convinced by it. He knew that it was and is important music. In fact, so strong and overwhelming was his conviction, that in that moment he convinced us all that Euryanthe was worth doing. And doing well. We had to give of our best. Because if HE was involved 100%, if HE was giving the piece his all, then we'd better do the same.

Within moments, we were all on the edge of our seats, being super-attentive, watching and listening in a way that we hadn't done for weeks. And the result? We were singing like a choir possessed. The intonation, the line, the blend, the articulation, the rhythmic attack – not to mention the notes themselves – they were all there.

It ended up being a hugely satisfying rehearsal. And a week later at the QEH we were part of an outstanding performance. But how did it happen? How could we, as a choir, go from being so lousy to so good in such a short period of time, in just a few minutes? What was it that took place in that rehearsal between 8.00pm and 8.30? When we started the evening we already knew the piece – the notes. And we also knew "how it goes". We certainly knew each other. So, what was different? Well, clearly, the only difference was Mark Elder. Everything else was the same. But how could he make such a difference? After all, he said almost nothing. There was no great motivational speech before his downbeat. There were no wise words trying to persuade us that Weber and "Euryanthe" are worthy of our attention.

There was nothing. But in that "nothing" there was everything. Somehow, he was able to galvanise – ie: lead – a group of singers to give far more than they believed they could, and in the process create something special. He worked magic, and I was mystified. I had no idea how Mark Elder did what he did. But ever since I've wanted to understand the basis of such technique and artistry because I had a hunch that such leadership skills and abilities are not just used and seen in the rarefied world of Classical music. Such skills are relevant everywhere; in our everyday worlds of domestic and family life, and also in the organisations and businesses that so many of us work in.

When we get Leadership right we create the potential to change the lives of those around us – our families, our work colleagues – in a special way. But, of course, we've all been on the receiving end of the opposite. And, if we're honest, we've all been guilty of doing the opposite.

So, my questions for you to reflect on are simple:

Who is your 'Sir Mark Elder'? Either within work or outside, who is a Leadership role model for you? Who do you take your inspiration from?

What makes them special? How have they influenced you? How have they changed your life? What skills and attitudes enable them to change people's lives? What can you learn – and borrow – from them?

How can you inspire the people you work with? What can you do to convince your colleagues that the task / project / assignment / problem that you're all working on is EXACTLY what you should all be doing?

Given that people are more affected by your BEHAVIOURS than your words, how can you convey this passion by your actions?

What would be the effect on your team's performance and morale if you could "do a Mark Elder" and lead with his level of conviction and vitality?

Variation 7 –
Are your people thriving?

The signs of outstanding leadership appear
primarily among the followers. Are the followers
reaching their potential? Are they learning?
Serving? Do they achieve the required results?
Do they change with grace? Manage conflict?

Max De Pree

If you ever want to see "Leadership" in action, in front of your very
eyes, I strongly recommend spending an evening listening to and
watching an orchestra. Even if you think that classical music is "not
your thing" I think you'll still be impressed by the extraordinary
technical accomplishment of what you see before you.

As I've mentioned in an earlier essay, there are actually a few smaller
Chamber orchestras that never have anyone standing in front of
them. As a group of musicians, they have chosen the path of self-
direction – "refugees from conductors" as Sir Neville Marriner used
to quip. But such groups are the exception. The majority of orchestras
do have a conductor standing in front of them, and it's these I want
to consider for the moment.

If you've ever watched an orchestra and wondered … "What do
conductors do?" then you're not alone. Regularly when chatting
about classical music and orchestras, I've been asked …"What are
conductors for?" … "Why are they there?" … "What is the point
of them?" … "Why do orchestras pay such big money to hire them
when the players hardly seem to even look at them?".

OK, such questions are slightly provocative and tongue-in-cheek.
But at the same time I think they're worth considering. The

person standing in front of the orchestra clearly has some purpose; someone thinks they're of value otherwise they wouldn't be there; they're presumably keeping the group together and providing encouragement. But is that it? Is that all they're there for? What else are they doing?

Perhaps if you could actually see what the orchestra sees – the front of the conductor, their face, their eyes – it might be easier to tell. But, as an audience member, you rarely do. All you see is their back.

Ciaran Fenton, a friend and colleague of mine who coaches corporate Boards, has a refreshingly no-nonsense approach when working with leaders. For him, the role of a leader is simple: "You're there to enable your people to thrive". That's it. Nothing more, nothing less.

In my experience, good conductors know this instinctively. They understand what we, the performers in front of them, need in order to succeed, and how they can help us achieve the desired results. As with any team there are things that performers find easy and things that we find difficult. But they're not always obvious. When looking at a score, skilful conductors have an uncanny awareness of what we will find tricky and need help with, and, on the other hand, what we can sort out for ourselves. They have a sixth sense for knowing when to step in and provide assistance. But they also know, often, more importantly, when to step back and keep quiet, and let us self-correct. As the conductor, Bernard Haitink, once said to a young student conductor: "Don't distract them. They're busy".

Sometimes what looks difficult on paper, on the score, is actually fairly straightforward. A section might look very challenging rhythmically, but if you can feel how it goes then the problem often evaporates. Likewise, a work can sound very dense and opaque harmonically but is actually far easier to perform than it sounds, especially if it sits well in the voice or lies well under the fingers.

Then again, the opposite can happen; pieces which at first glance should be sight-readable, in practice are far more demanding. Often, very slow pieces, which pose no challenge when it comes to the notes themselves or the rhythms, can be uncommonly strenuous and require practice to develop the necessary stamina.

Frequently, the difficulty is not so much to do with the music, but rather the practicalities of performing; just hearing your colleagues. Ideally choirs are arranged in compact blocks, so that the sopranos, altos, tenors and basses are sitting together in groups. But this doesn't always happen. I once sang a concert in St Paul's Cathedral where we were not only strung out in two long lines but we were also mixed up – ie: we were NOT standing next to another member of our own voice part. Given the strange acoustics of St Paul's, this meant that we couldn't even hear them. For the whole of the sixty minutes the only two voices I did hear were the soprano and alto immediately adjacent to me. When the basses were singing together it was as if I was singing a solo. (As it happens, I'm told that the resultant blend heard in the nave was excellent, but from where we were performing, right under the dome, no sound was coming back and it was extremely disconcerting.)

In orchestras, it can be worse. Because of the larger numbers involved, there is the combination of both bigger physical spaces and also separation between players. And the volume of sound is greater. Let's imagine the score dictates that the French horns and the cellos need to "duet" and blend. But if the whole horn section is playing at once it can be impossible for them to hear anything outside of their immediate surroundings. They might be able to see the cellos but there's no chance of hearing them. So how can they possibly play together, play "as one"?

And then there are situations when it's possible to hear colleagues fairly clearly, but the problem is "when". Cathedrals provide one of the largest spaces for musicians. Most of the time the choir and organ are in close proximity. But during some services the choir goes "walk-about" and processes to the farthest reaches of the building.

At these points organist and choir can be sixty or seventy metres apart, a distance that creates a significant time lag in the sound. Playing and singing together under these circumstances is fraught with problems.

And then what if you attempt to squeeze a full symphony orchestra into a cathedral. Large as these buildings are, they weren't designed as concert halls and so it's likely that some players – often the percussionists – will find themselves tucked away behind a pillar, out of sight of both the audience and most of their colleagues.

In every one of these situations the possibility of the performers "not thriving" is very real. Good as they are, they need help. And the only person who can provide that help, the only one who can come to the rescue, is the conductor. They're the only one who has the overall view, the only person who can hear everything in balance.

So, my questions for you to reflect on are simple:

As a leader, exactly how do you help your people thrive?

When did you last "stand back" and let your team self-correct? What was the outcome? What did it do for team morale?

Who are the people in your team who are on the periphery, tucked away behind the proverbial "pillar", or unable to hear or see their colleagues? How can you help them contribute?

How can you ensure nobody ever asks "What are you for? What do you do for your team"?

Variation 8 –
What it takes to Trust

"Trust is the glue of life. It's the most essential
ingredient in effective communication.
It's the foundational principle that
holds all relationships."

Stephen Covey

There are many models which attempt to identify and describe the behaviours we see in good teams. But every one of those models has one trait in common. Trust. In every model it's there somewhere. For Patrick Lencioni, in his highly readable book "The Five Dysfunctions of a Team", it's centre-stage. For him it's the very foundation upon which organisational teamwork is built.

Trust is certainly a key element in the lives of musicians. Performing 'live', which is what many professional musicians do day in and day out, is fraught with dangers and risks – the risks of failure, of making mistakes which are all too public, of letting your colleagues down, of not being asked back for another job (almost all musicians are freelance and habitually insecure about their futures). Naturally, they practise and rehearse assiduously to minimise the risks but nevertheless the hazards remain. Every evening it's a "high wire act" which takes them to their limits – though hopefully not beyond – in the search of that elusive magic, the magic of a great performance. And all this is done in front of a paying audience, in the public arena, literally "in the spotlight".

Trust is one of those words that we all use from time to time. We all "know what we mean" by it. And yet, like Leadership, it can be surprisingly difficult to pin down, perhaps because it has so many strands and depends on whom we're trusting.

Trusting colleagues

I remember chatting to a colleague about this. His background was very different from mine: he'd had years in the military culminating in a period serving in the SAS so I was interested in his perspective and whether it may have any relevance to the concert hall. Certainly, he knew plenty about "performing" in the presence of risk and danger. I asked him what it was that made the Special Air Service special. Without hesitation he replied "It's all about Trust. When you start training and then eventually go out on active service, you're always in a small unit, just a few guys. And in that unit, surrounded by danger everywhere, there's no space for 'doubt'. You have to be able to trust your colleagues 100%. You must trust them more than you have ever trusted anyone else. Because one day, almost literally, your life may be in their hands." There was a pause before he continued. "That's why the training takes so long. Yes, partly it's to build fitness and stamina and mental resilience, but just as important is the time we spend together, getting to know each other, and the trust that comes from that. It's a slow process. You don't build that closeness in a half-day workshop!"

Trust, then, is fundamental to the Special Forces. But it's vital for the professional musician too. Admittedly, a concert, however high-profile, is never a case of 'life-or-death' – let's not kid ourselves that this is the SAS – but nevertheless there are parallels that can be drawn. One is being able to trust colleagues. For me, for example, in one of the groups I perform with there is a person that I always like to sit next to. After 10 years or so of countless rehearsals and concerts together I know I can rely on him completely, not just to 'get it right' (of course he does that), but more importantly I can rely on him to take risks, to 'go for it', to seek out that magic. As it happens, we're not best mates. I'd never choose to spend time with him outside of our musical relationship. But, as a performing colleague, he is outstandingly reliable. I know I can trust him 100%. And that's extremely liberating.

Trust between the Leader and Performer

But for musicians it's not just about trusting those immediately around you. If there's a conductor involved then it's vital that you can trust them, trust that they'll do what they've promised to do. Concerts are a very public test for performers, however experienced they might be. The players are the ones putting their necks on the line, the ones who will look stupid if things go awry. They're the ones who create the sound, the ones in the spotlight, the ones whom the audience hear. By contrast, the conductor is the only person on stage who makes no sound, the only one who remains silent throughout the concert. If they make a mistake the chances are that the audience will be none the wiser. If the Trumpet comes in early, on the other hand, then it's a different matter.

But this trust has two sides. Trusting that the conductor will do what they said they'd do – give a clear down-beat here, give a cut-off there – is one side of the coin. But what an orchestra or band or choir want at least in equal measure is to know that they are trusted by the conductor, that they are trusted enough to be stretched. A professional orchestra, like any elite group, wants to be pushed, it wants to be driven hard. So, does the conductor trust the group enough to loosen the reins? Musicians can sense trust (or lack of it) within moments. During the initial run-through of a piece the players will be looking to see if the conductor is willing to let things go, to overlook certain rough edges and blemishes. Does the conductor trust the players will be able to self-correct second time around? Do they trust that the group instinctively knows a) what needs to be corrected and b) has the necessary skills to do it? Do they trust the players enough that they don't need to assert their authority too early in the relationship? And then, later on, when it comes to the performance, can they trust the players to follow them come-what-may? Do they trust enough to push the group to its limits? And do they trust that, if they've miscalculated, that the group will be able to recover the situation and get them out of the mess?

Trusting themselves

And finally, performers have to trust themselves. They must have total confidence that the 1000's of hours of practice and rehearsal will see them through; that their technique will hold up under pressure; that their concentration will withstand the inevitable distractions of "live" performance; that their memory won't fail them; that when the time comes they are able to rise to the challenge, throw caution to the wind and do something unexpected; that they can go as "close to the edge" as they dare; that they are willing to take all the risks necessary to create magic.

And, as well as trusting that they will be able to "perform" on the night, even more important is that they must trust and have total belief that what they're doing is worthwhile, that they have something valid to say.

Producing anything worthwhile, be it on the concert stage or in the organisational Board Room, is dangerous and risky. You must be prepared to face your fears full-on – your fears of failure, of humiliation, of inadequacy ... in essence, your fear of your own vulnerability.

So, my questions for you to reflect on are these:

What does being vulnerable mean to you? What are some of the perceived dangers you associate with being vulnerable? And what might be some of the potential benefits?

When you think of a team you lead or are part of, when is it easy and difficult for you to show your vulnerability? When do you find it easy to trust the individuals in your team, and when is it still a challenge?

What do you need from your closest colleagues in order to trust them and be vulnerable with them? And what do they need in order to trust and be vulnerable with you? (NB: It's different for each of us.)

What would be the hardest thing for you to acknowledge to your senior colleagues? What would be difficult for you to disclose in open forum?

How easy would it be for you to expose your weaknesses and admit to your peers … "I don't know what to do" or "I feel I'm out of my depth" or "I'm completely struggling with this" or "I really need your help"? If you were able to say these things what might the benefits be for you and the team? If you ARE able to say them, what have been the benefits?

Variation 9 –
Life at a Distance

"Your assumptions are your windows
on the world. Scrub them off every once
in a while, or the light won't come in."

Isaac Asimov

As we've seen previously, one of the gifts which separates humans from other animals derives from the structure of our brains, and in particular our frontal lobes. As a result of our biology, we have an ability to detach ourselves from the immediate, and see ourselves "in time". We, as humans, are able to look forward in time and make choices about what might be. To a degree we are able to over-ride our instincts, our programming, and determine our future in the way that other animals cannot. Simultaneously, we also have an ability to look back in time and see what was, see where we've been, see where we've come from, and perhaps learn from our past.

Studying our ancestry can make us aware of many things, the first being simply just how many ancestors we actually each have. The number, without being too precise, is LOTS. Think about it: every one of us has had two parents, and four grand-parents, and 8 great grand-parents and so on all the way back through the centuries. That quickly adds up. Three generations – 14 ancestors – take us back about 90 years or so. With twenty generations we're back to the 14th century, and by then the number of our ancestors has become hundreds-of-thousands. OK, they may not all have lived that long necessarily. But, they all lived long enough to procreate, to pass on their genes. Regardless of how far back I choose to look – whether it be thousands or tens-of-thousands or hundreds-of-thousands of years all the way back to when we roamed the plains of Africa – the one thing I know about every one of my ancestors (and your ancestors too for that matter), is that, without exception, they all survived long enough to breed successfully. I think that's pretty remarkable. Hundreds of thousands of them, and every single one made it!

Survival is at the heart of our lives. For all creatures – mammals, birds, reptiles, insects – life, at its most fundamental, is about two things: reproduction and survival. And since we humans are mammals, it's no different for us. Survival of the species means that the majority of individuals must reproduce, and they must survive long enough to do so. But for our early ancestors walking the African savannah there was an immediate challenge. How could they tell whether an approaching stranger was a potential mate or a potential threat? How could they decide, from say 200 metres away, whether the person was to be welcomed or attacked, whether they are a friend or foe? At such moments, there's little time to evaluate the situation. The potential danger is only seconds away. And so humans developed numerous ways of assessing other people, clues to help them weigh up possible risks from others. We've been doing it for tens-of-thousands of years. And, even though the risks may now be different from those faced by our ancestors, we continue to do so. We all take shortcuts with regard to trying to understand others. Of course, we all know that we shouldn't evaluate others prematurely – "Don't judge a book by its cover". And we also understand that in a perfect world we should get to know other people in depth, be they a new client or a new member of the team or a casual acquaintance. But, who's got the time to do that with everyone? And besides, haven't we all said at some time "I know what they're like. I've met people like that before"?

We all make assumptions. And we all generalise. In fact, it's an extremely useful skill to be able to generalise because if we couldn't then we would have to learn everything afresh every time. For example: you go to meet a new client for the first time. At their offices you open a door. Now, this might sound obvious, but how did you know it was a door? After all, it's your first time in the building

119

and you've never seen that particular door before. How could you be certain that it was a door? Well, you couldn't be 100% certain. But you have seen plenty of other things that are like it, you've seen plenty of other doors in your life, and so you draw on that experience – you generalise – and conclude that this thing also happens to be a door. As the saying goes "If it looks like a duck, swims like a duck, and quacks like a duck, then it probably is a duck". And most of the time you get such abductive inferences right. (For an amusing example of someone getting it wrong, when their inferences were incorrect, then take a look on YouTube for "George W. Bush Can't Open the Door").

Just as we make assumptions and inferences about doors and things that look like doors, we also make assumptions and generalise about people. We have to. Regardless of how open-minded we are, we haven't got time to reinvent the wheel every second of the day, so we take short-cuts and use "educated guesses" to steer us in the right direction, to give us clues about how someone should be dealt with, what they might be good at, what they might be weak at, what drives and motivates them, what they need. Over the centuries we've developed and formalised countless models and "typologies" to help us assess people. Understandably, as fashions change, these various models have fallen in and out of favour. In the past we've categorised people according to the size of their Bodies, the shape of their Faces, the breadth and length of their Hands and Fingers, their height, even their Blood group! Many cultures have seen connections between dates of birth and behaviours – "I'm a Gemini" … "I'm born in the Year of the Horse" – whilst some have gone as far as suggesting that there are connections between Race and certain character traits. Clearly these latter suggestions are now very non-PC – the idea of categorising people according to their ethnicity is anathema to many. And yet, at the same time, whenever I mention that I've worked with groups and individuals around the globe, I'm struck by how many people ask what the sessions are like, the assumptions being that these coaching workshops and 1-2-1s in Chicago or Shanghai or Johannesburg or Helsinki will somehow be different from each other. Since the attendees are from different ethnic backgrounds, there's a belief that they may act differently, that they will be more or less open, more or less willing to share, want more or less interaction, want more or less speed, that the sessions will be more or less fun. I'm not saying this is right or wrong. I'm simply suggesting that we all categorise and make assumptions more than we might like to think.

In more recent decades, perhaps as our Left Hemispheres have become over-confident, we've attempted to add some "science" to this process of categorisation. The number of psychometrics attempting to classify and measure people's behaviours has grown significantly. In our workplaces we're now keener than ever to know whether our colleagues/our boss/our peers/our direct reports/our clients are Curious or Cautious? Efficient or Easy-going? Outgoing or Reserved? Nervous or Confident? Compassionate or Detached? We are no longer satisfied simply with measuring someone's IQ, we now want to quantify their emotional intelligence. We relentlessly gather ever more information and data in an attempt to establish "Are they like us? Can we connect? Can we work together? Will they fit in to our group?".

I want to stress that there is nothing inherently wrong or bad about psychometrics – indeed, I've been employing a number of them in my work for over 20 years. Used properly, such tools can facilitate and deepen conversations remarkably quickly. But it's essential to remember that they are just that – "tools". We must always be aware of their limitations, and their role. They are not "the end", they are simply the "means to an end". As Iain McGilchrist might say, they can be a wonderful Servant but they are a very poor Master. And, whilst they can act like a compass and perhaps offer us some rules to follow, it's worth heeding the advice of Carl Jung when he cautioned that "Everyone is an exception to the rules".

So, my questions for you to reflect on are these:

When it comes to people, what are some of the rules you've lived by to try and understand others? What are some assumptions that you've made?

What mental models – politically correct or otherwise! – have you used or created to help you make judgements about people?

What prejudices are you prepared to own up to and admit to yourself? (It's OK, you don't have to share these with anyone else!)

When did these rules and assumptions and models serve you well? How did they help you "survive"?

When did they not help you? How did they get in your way? When have you "done a George W Bush" and made a wrong assumption?

What was the effect of this mistake on you? What was the cost? What was the effect on the other person? What would you do differently now?

Where did these assumptions come from? If they originated in your childhood, what has changed for you since then?

If you accept that "Everyone is an exception to the rules" how might that help you see people differently?

Variation 10 –
The Leader as Psychologist

"Emotional intelligence, more than any
other factor, more than I.Q. or expertise, accounts
for 85% to 90% of success at work.
I.Q. is a threshold competence. You need it,
but it doesn't make you a star.
Emotional intelligence can."

Warren G. Bennis

The first couple of decades of the 20th century saw some major advances in both the sciences and social sciences. Albert Einstein turned the world of Physics upside down in 1905 and then again in 1915 when he published first his Special Theory and then his General Theory of Relativity. In many ways Carl Jung's book, "Psychological Types", had a similarly seismic effect in the realm of psychology, offering a holistic model to help us understand why we behave as we do.

Both men's outputs demonstrate the power of imagination and ideas. As Walter Isaacson described in the NY Times, "Einstein relished what he called Gedankenexperimente, ideas that he twirled around in his head rather than in a lab. That's what teachers call daydreaming, but if you're Einstein you get to call them Gedankenexperimente." One of Einstein's first and perhaps most famous thought-experiments was when he wondered "What would it be like to ride on a beam of light?" – ie: How would the world appear if I could travel at the speed of light? This seemingly simple question eventually gave rise to the Special Theory, which focused not only on the speed of light but also on the notions of time and mass, and gave us the most famous scientific equation: $E = MC^2$.

A decade later, in the General Theory, Einstein suggested the extraordinary idea that Gravity could affect the passage of light, even though light has no mass. Whilst experiments carried out a few years later revealed that light can indeed be affected by gravity and can be bent by planets, and whilst astronomers have now found evidence of Black Holes – objects so massive that nothing, perhaps not even light can escape – it's important to remember that for Einstein the theories came first. His work went on in his head, in his imagination.

The same could be said of Carl Jung. Nowadays, psychological researchers looking for patterns in the ways we all behave have powerful computers at their disposal, and are able to carry out factor analysis on vast data sets of hundreds of thousands of people. By contrast, the hard data that Jung had at his disposal was miniscule, coming as it did from a mere few hundred patients that he worked with during his career. These case studies were undoubtedly useful, but perhaps even more important was Jung's remarkable ability to "look within", to study himself, to examine his own drives and motivations, to become self-aware.

In many ways the most remarkable aspect of Einstein's work is that, one hundred years on, it is still relevant. In fact, it's more than relevant. It still underpins much of modern physics and how we view the world. Of course, it's been developed and built upon by successive generations of physicists. But the fundamentals still stand.

Likewise with the work of Carl Jung. The basic building-blocks of personality which he proposed way back in 1921 still have wide acceptance. Naturally they have been augmented and developed and adapted over the years but for many practitioners Jung is still at the heart of self-development and understanding people.

Whenever we're leading people – whether it's a team, a client meeting, or simply a 1-2-1 colleague review – it's self-evident that we need to understand those people in front of us so that we can then recognise why we might sometimes have misunderstandings. When addressing questions such as "How are we different from each other? And why do we experience misunderstandings?" Jung believed that, once we stripped away all the superficial differences, there were three major factors at play. Firstly, he saw a big difference in where we focus – in particular, where we place our energy and from where we derive our energy. Secondly, he saw a big difference in the way people make decisions – some focusing on the task, others focusing more on the people. Then thirdly, he saw a significant difference in the way people perceive the world – some tending first to see "the whole", others tending to see the details that make up that whole.

Our Attitude to the world

When it comes to how we attend to the world, how we pay attention, Jung observed that some people focus very strongly on the outside. And not only do they prefer to attend to the outside world, to externalities, but they are also energised by it. They derive energy from interacting with people and objects and things around them.

By contrast, he noted that the primary focus of other people was more internal, that they focused more on their inner world and were energised by their own subjective experience.

The terms he used to describe these two ways of attending to the world – these two Attitudes – were Extraversion and Introversion. Whilst these two words have entered our everyday vocabulary, I think it's fair to say that they're not seen and valued equally. Certainly our Western society has a bias towards and promotes Extraversion, with introverts often being encouraged to "come out of their shell" because they're thought of as being "shy". Jung, however, was adamant that these two attitudes are absolutely of equal importance for our own mental wellbeing. And he was also clear that we all experience both, that this is a case of "both/and" not "either/or". We all clearly live in the outside world, and interact with others from time to time. And by the same token, we all have an "inner life" and spend time there too. Introversion is in no way inferior to Extraversion, and neither is it an absence of Extraversion. Whilst the two attitudes are clearly related, Introversion should be seen as a distinct aspect of our personality.

Given Introversion's inward focus, some of the behaviours we commonly associate with it are:

- Being quieter and more private
- Enjoying one's own company
- Being more reserved and reflective
- Preferring "depth" – having fewer interests and fewer relationships but taking them deeper

Extraversion's outward focus, on the other hand, means it is associated more with:

- Being quite talkative and open
- Enjoying the company of others
- Being outgoing and outspoken
- Preferring "breadth" – having lots of interests and pastimes, lots of friends and acquaintances

As I've already suggested, reflecting on these two very distinctive ways of relating to the world may give us some clues as to why we misunderstand others. We'll explore this more at the end of the essay.

The way we make our Decisions

The second major difference that Carl Jung saw in people was to do with how they make decisions, and what the basis is for those decisions. In popular parlance this could be characterised by "Are you a Head person or a Heart person". We might paraphrase that question by further asking "Do you prefer to make decisions objectively, based on facts and data, or more subjectively, based on what you like?" Or using Jungian terminology, we could ask "Do you have a preference for 'Thinking' or 'Feeling' when making decisions?"

When we are using our Thinking preference, some of the behaviours that might come to the fore are:

- Being task-focused and concentrating on getting stuff done
- Analysing data and being logical
- Seeing life as a competition and wanting to win
- Having an ability to be detached and impersonal

When we are using our Feeling preference the behaviours we are more likely to witness are:

- Being focused on the other person and our relationship
- Subjectively bringing our own likes and dislikes to the fore
- Being personal and considerate
- Having a desire to connect and be involved

As with Introversion and Extraversion, we all do both: when we make our decisions we all want to get the job done, and we all care about people, about our colleagues. Yes, we may use one approach first, but we will use both. Nevertheless, there is often a misconception about Thinking and Feeling. Even though this pair of preferences is unambiguously about "HOW we make decisions" – for Jung, this was the Rational Function – it can sometimes be interpreted incorrectly as "DO we or DON'T we make decisions?". When we decide using a strong Thinking preference we study information and analyse data, and there is a clear logic to our process. It's all very objective. And, perhaps most importantly, we can easily articulate and communicate our objective logic to others. When we decide using a strong Feeling preference, on the other hand, it's rather different. It's difficult to be as convincing. Our decisions can appear rather vague and woolly.

Let's think about cars for a moment. Imagine I'm trying to explain to you why I've bought a Honda rather than a Ford. To many people my explanation will carry more weight if I've obviously "done my homework", if I focus on verifiable data such the MPG and Running costs, the Performance, the Price and Specification. If, instead, I say the reason for my choice is "I simply prefer the Honda", in some ways that decision seems less robust, perhaps even less valid. It may actually elicit a question "Why do you prefer it?" … to which the answer is even more simply "Because I do".

As it turns out, there's a wealth of psychological research to show that we ALL make our decisions subjectively – ie: we all use our Feeling preference first – but then some of us like to back up that decision with supporting, objective data – ie: using our Thinking preference second. It's further suggested that people who claim to do otherwise – "I always make decisions logically" – are in fact just moving from stage 1 to stage 2 at lightning speed.

As with our attitudes of Introversion and Extraversion, Thinking and Feeling can cause significant misunderstandings. These will be explored a little further on.

A matter of Perception

The third pair of preferences that Carl Jung observed – preferences that once again differentiate us – was to do with perception, with how people perceive, with how we view the world. Using the modern vernacular we might ask "Are you a 'Big Picture' person or a 'Detail' person"? In other words, do you first tend and prefer to see "the whole", or do you first see the individual elements that go to make up that whole? Some people when they "see" – be it a picture, a landscape, a "team", an opportunity, or some other situation – actually prefer to take in the entirety. And for them their entirety includes not just "what is there", but also "what is not there", what is less obvious. It's as if instead of "reading the lines" they prefer to "read between the lines".

Other people, however, absorb things in a very different way. They see exactly what is there, in forensic detail. They are truly expert at "reading the lines". Instinctively what they see first are individual pieces, separate items of information. Only once they have enough of these individual bits, these isolated pieces, do they consolidate them and begin to notice patterns. And eventually they will build them, rather like a mosaic, into a single entity, a picture of reality. Until that happens, though, it's a world of unconnected details.

Jung referred to these two disparate modes of perceiving as Intuition and Sensation.

When we are using our Intuition our perspective tends to be:

- Comprehensive and holistic
- Imaginative and creative
- Spontaneous and unpredictable
- Often focused on the future and on intangibles

When we have a preference for Sensation, on the other hand, our attention is on:

- Specifics and minutiae
- Being realistic and practical
- Structure and consistency
- The here-and-now and the tangible

These two preferences are hugely important, not just because they are about how we see the world, but because they are at the very heart of how we communicate with each other, how we influence our colleagues.

Let's say you want to convince someone of the benefits of getting involved in a particular project with you. If you have a preference for Intuition you would probably start by painting the future for them – "This is where we could be in a year's time, in two years, in three years!". The language you would use would probably be imaginative and creative. You would focus on the "big picture", and consequently be rather vague on details, assuming that they will be able to "fill in the gaps". And you would be comfortable going off on tangents, talking around the subject, in a spontaneous, free-flowing way.

All of which would be terrific if that's their style too. But what if they have a preference for Sensation? Painting the future for them holds no attraction, because they tend to focus on the here-and-now and the immediate next-steps. For them, "This is where we'll be in three years' time" is not exciting or persuasive in the least. It's just a pointless pipe-dream. Likewise, your imaginative, big-picture, blue-sky thinking will fall on deaf ears, because it's way too vague. There are no details supporting the idea. There's nothing tangible for them to get hold of. And, finally, as for going off on tangents, well, this is perhaps the most irritating aspect of all. Moving from idea to idea might be flexible and creative to you. But to them it suggests a hopelessly chaotic mind. And an approach that is doomed to fail.

And so, they don't come on board. NOT because it's a lousy idea. But simply because you didn't communicate it properly. You communicated your way, not theirs. You didn't speak their language, the language of Sensation.

So, my questions for you to reflect on are these:

When it comes to Perception and how you see the world, do you consider yourself more of a "big picture" or "detail" person ... as a "future oriented" or "here and now" sort of person? Thinking of a time when a friend or colleague was successful in "getting you onboard", what did they focus on? How did they manage to win you over?

Thinking of a time when you have not got your message across as well as you wanted, how were you trying to persuade your audience? What were you focusing on? What would your audience have preferred to hear? How do you think they perceived you in that moment? What did that misjudgement cost you?

When it comes to making decisions, are you more of a "head" or a "heart" person ... are you more task-focused or people-focused? What are the advantages of your particular preference? When has it served you well?

When has your preference not served you so well? Describe what happened? What was your approach? What did you not do that the other person wanted you to consider? What could you have done differently? How might the outcome have been better?

In what situations do you show the extraverted side of your personality? How comfortable are you in these times? What do we see? How does it help you? Are you ever guilty of overplaying your Extraversion, of using it too much?

When do you show the Introverted side of your personality? How comfortable are you in these circumstances? What do we see? How does your Introversion help you? Do you ever overplay it? How does it ever get in your way?

Variation 11 –
The Seduction of Reduction

"If we believe something does not exist unless we measure it, then we put aside: love, feeling, intuition, art and philosophy."

Peter Block

Where is "the music" in a piece of music? Is it possible to isolate what it is that affects us so much? How does a piece, whether it be a love song by Adele or a prelude of Bach, work its magic? How does it create the exhilarations, the tears, the sense of despair, the joys? How is it possible for music to sometimes take us to "another level"?

When we ask "Where is the music?" the temptation is to answer that it must lie in the notes themselves. After all, what else is there? But, actually, can that be the case? Individual notes are meaningless. If you go to a piano and press down a key all you've done is create some sound. A single note by itself isn't music. It has the potential to be music only when there are several notes together, when the initial single note is connected to other notes, either "horizontally" as part of a melody, or "vertically" as part of a chord.

If, then, you only start to get music when there's more than one note, it's been suggested (supposedly by Debussy and Mozart, both of whom should know about these things) that actually "the music is in the spaces between the notes." But, again, can that be the whole answer? The "spaces between" – ie: often the "silences" – are just that, silent. In the same way that a single note can't be music, neither can a period of silence.

Surely a more likely answer is that it's not a case of "either/or", but rather that the music somehow lies in a combination of the two, in the notes as they exist within the whole. Whenever we encounter things in their context, whenever we see the gestalt, there is an inevitable aliveness and vitality to our experience. But equally inevitable is that this very energy and vibrancy disappears as soon as entities are examined in isolation, whenever they are removed from their context.

This is the challenge we face whenever we create maps and models of the world. Maps and models can be extremely useful. It's hard to imagine life without them. They allow us to distil our chaotic, lived experience down to a number of key elements, which we can then categorise and compare, and examine in detail. As we focus on the parts, we're able to home in on certain features and ignore others that we deem to be of lesser interest and use to us. And, hence, we're able to manipulate and utilise and control the world around us.

By definition, maps simplify. They omit far more than they include. Think of the road maps in your car. The terrain you're driving through, the view out of the window, isn't like the map at all. On the road map there are no hills, probably no buildings shown, there are certainly no trees, and it's possible that some landmarks have been omitted altogether. But whilst the map ignores most of the details – actually, because the map ignores most of the details – it's extremely useful. As long as it's "accurate enough" then it will enable you to get from A to B with some certainty. That's the map's great strength. It includes a few significant details and avoids the "clutter" inherent in the whole.

But, whilst the simplicity of maps is seductively attractive, it's all too easy to forget that most of the whole, most of "what is", is missing. And so often, "what is" is precisely what makes the thing alive and magical. Invariably, our maps of the world omit the very things that make our experience special.

As I've already mentioned, while studying Biology at school I dissected a frog. As a result, I learned a good deal about the frog's physiology and anatomy – its digestive system, nervous system, respiratory system, skeletal structure and so on. But sadly, in the process of reducing the frog down to its constituent parts, what I ended up with was a dead frog. Which was unfortunate because the very thing that I wanted to know more about was actually a living frog. Of course, it can be useful to know what the constituent parts of a frog are, but it's also crucial to recognise that a living frog is a lot more than the sum of its constituent parts. There's a certain "froginess" that no amount of dissection can capture or convey.

Likewise, when we dissect a poem or a piece of music, when we study word-by-word or note-by-note what is going on, the danger is that we learn everything about the poem or piece except what it is that makes it unique and magical. Just as previously we're left with a dead frog, in the case of the poem or piece of music the risk is that all that remains are lifeless marks on a page where once there was energy and insight.

And so it is in the world of work. Models are ubiquitous and have been designed to cover every aspect of organisational life – from Leadership to Change; from Strategy to Finance; from Marketing to People and Behaviour. Like many tools they can be powerful, and when used elegantly they have the potential to be a force for good. But if used clumsily and out of context then it can be just the reverse. Take, for example, the Kubler-Ross Change Curve which postulates different stages that someone might travel through in the face of significant change. As with the road map mentioned earlier, this provides a very general plan of the "change terrain". But, as a leader, it will tell you precious little about the specific lived experience and the support needed by a member of your team who is struggling. As always, the model has omitted so much, almost everything of value.

The British philosopher, Gilbert Ryle, coined the term "category mistake" to highlight those occasions when either we try to compare things which really should not be compared, or we use a methodology (eg: creating targets for care services within the

NHS) that's inappropriate. If you're dealing with a machine then a mechanistic, reductionist mindset, where 2+2 always equals 4, and where individual parts can be examined in isolation is perfectly legitimate. But when you're studying people – and, let's be clear, that's all your organisation is: it's simply a collection of people – then you need a different approach, one that recognises the importance of context.

When you think of the team you lead and the organisation you're a part of, then attempting to reduce it down to a list of its component parts or packing it into a 4-box matrix can often cause more problems than it solves. Yes, it's neat and tidy. And it's ever so convenient. But as I've previously mentioned, the so-called "seduction of reduction" is a dangerous thing. Your team is a living, breathing entity, and is so much more than any model can suggest.

So, my questions for you to reflect on are these:

What are some of the models you use in your leadership world?
What are you hoping to discover by using them?

As a leader, when is it appropriate to use each model? And when is it not?

What are the limitations of the various models you use?
When have you been guilty of a "category mistake"?

When have you used a model to help you try and understand your organisational world, only to end up with a lifeless – and useless – "dead frog"?

What could you have done differently?
How could you have included the context, and thereby examined the whole?
How could you have examined it AND kept it alive?!

What is the "froginess", the essence of your team or organisation, that makes it so special? Is it really possible to articulate what it is? Could it be measured in any meaningful way? (Don't worry if you can't articulate it clearly or measure it. That's OK!).

Variation 12 –
Preparation and Practice

"Give me six hours to chop down a tree and I will
spend the first four sharpening the axe. "

Abraham Lincoln (attrib)

When we go to a performance at, say, London's Royal Festival Hall,
whether it's a solo recital or an orchestral concert it's tempting to
think of those two hours in front of the paying audience as being
what the performers on stage do for a living. And, of course, in one
sense it is. But what needs to be stressed is that it is only a part of
their job. And, often, it's a rather small part.

John Lill, the distinguished English pianist, has had a significant
international career playing with the world's greatest orchestras.
At the same time he's enjoyed playing in smaller, out-of-the-way
venues, where those attending are perhaps less experienced, less
sophisticated. He likes to tell the story that it was after one such
concert that he was asked by a well-meaning organiser "And what
do you do during the day, then?". We can only assume that they
believed that playing the Schumann Fantasy and the Beethoven
'Hammerklavier' needed little if any preparation.

The reality, in fact, is precisely the opposite. The public hours spent
on stage, when performers do what we assume they do for a living,
probably amount to less than 10% of their working schedule. The
life of a concert pianist is mostly one of preparation and practice,
a solitary life of endless polishing and study. It doesn't matter that
they may have known the work in question for 30 years, that they've
played it 200 times before, and that last night's performance was
received with rapturous applause. Today is another day. There can
be no room for complacency. Every corner of the piece must be

examined afresh, every page of the score put under the microscope for the umpteenth time, in a never-ending search for excellence. Sometimes, just moments before walking onto the platform, you can hear a pianist back stage going over some awkward detail on the Green Room upright. Of course, they already know the piece, and they can get through it, and will give a perfectly acceptable "professional" performance come what may. But refining and honing their craft are as much a part of their daily routine as brushing their teeth. Preparation is what they do.

It's no different, of course, in the world of elite sport. Manchester City, as a team, play way fewer than 100 hours per annum. And yet they are on the training ground every day. Heavyweight boxer, Anthony Joshua, averages only 2 or 3 bouts a year, each lasting little more than half-an-hour. But he is forever in the gym. And while the total length of Usain Bolt's performances were counted in seconds, he was on the practice track every day in the run-up to a major race. For all of these people, life is synonymous with preparation.

And, as with music and elite sport, so it is in other areas of our more everyday worlds. A painter/decorator spends remarkably little time with a paintbrush in hand. The majority of their effort is spent on getting themselves "ready" – stripping old paintwork, removing defective wall coverings, repairing damaged plasterwork, filling cracks, sanding uneven woodwork, hanging lining paper, priming new surfaces. Only then, once all these stages of preparation are complete, do they become "painters/decorators" as most of us would think of the term.

This focus on preparation has an interesting consequence. And that is that you have to love (or at least, learn to love) this aspect of the job in order to be successful long-term. Because that's what the job is really about. Naturally, a concert artist should enjoy the act of "public performance" (though some don't!), but even more, they must love the time spent alone, the endless hours of re-evaluation of a work, the perennial study of a masterpiece. Likewise, a professional sportsman such as Anthony Joshua must relish the regular training sessions and workouts in the gym. And our painter/decorator must be able to thrive on a daily routine of repairing, sanding and priming. Because that is the true nature of their jobs.

There's a parallel here in Stephen Covey's The 7 Habits of Highly Effective People in which Habit #7 is called "Sharpen the Saw." Covey uses the parable of a woodcutter who is sawing for several days straight and is becoming less and less productive. The process of cutting – of endless "doing" – dulls the blade, and so the solution is that the saw needs to be sharpened regularly. (If only the woodcutter had listened to Abraham Lincoln!)

As an organisational leader, you will know this. It's obvious. And it makes sense. And yet, organisational life often conspires against us. Most people have experienced at some point working so hard that their productivity begins to fall off.

Common wisdom suggests taking a break, maybe even going on holiday. But that actually isn't sharpening the saw — it's putting the saw down. And when you put down a blunt blade for a while, the blade will still be blunt when you pick it up again, even if it's two weeks later after a trip to Barbados.

No. Sharpening the saw is actually an activity, just as the parable suggests.

So, my questions for you to reflect on are these:

What does "preparation and practice" look like in your leadership world?

As a leader, how do you "sharpen your various blades" – your skills, your knowledge, your mind, your physical and emotional well-being?

What is the current ratio for you and those you lead between "preparation" and "doing"?

As a leader, how might you allocate more time to "preparation" and "sharpening the blade"? What might some benefits be? What is the cost to you of working with a "blunt blade"?

Is your annual "1–day Teambuilding offsite" really adequate? How might the members of your team allocate more time to "preparation" and "sharpening the blade"? What might some benefits be?

Variation 13 – Believing in yourself

"It is not the mountain we conquer, but ourselves."

Edmund Hillary (attrib)

I remember a distinguished actor once remarking that every day as she travelled to the theatre for the evening's performance she felt sick and was terrified. And she began wondering how many other professions were like that. Who else, if any, suffers such paralysing fear on an almost daily basis?

The assumption here is that going on stage in front of hundreds of people and playing a complicated theatrical part for several hours – and doing it all from memory – is terrifying. And, of course, for most of us it would be: we've all heard that for Joe Public the "Fear of Public Speaking" supposedly out-ranks the "Fear of Dying". So, even if in some way we could walk onto the stage, the chance of remembering and uttering our lines correctly is slim indeed.

But as we know, there are plenty of people – most professional performers, in fact – who CAN walk onto a theatrical or musical stage and perform at their best. So for me, whilst her question is interesting and thought-provoking, actually I'm far more intrigued by those actors and musicians who ARE able overcome those feelings that would cripple the rest of us. How do they do what they do? Because if we can figure that out then maybe that forthcoming presentation to the Board or a pitch to a prospective new client won't be quite so scary. Maybe it might even be more successful.

To be sure, performing takes a particular personality: it's certainly not for everyone. In the music world, at the extremes there are those who play as soloists, the people who get their names on the posters, the people whom we "go to see". Often, in the Classical music arena, they're there to play the solo part in one of the great romantic piano or violin concertos, during which they have a role that is almost gladiatorial, "the one versus the many". At other times the music making is maybe on a smaller, more intimate, scale. Either way, however, the demands can be extraordinarily high.

Back in 2008, over a period of barely three weeks, I saw the pianist (and conductor) Daniel Barenboim give a series of 8 recitals at London's Royal Festival Hall, during which he played all of Beethoven's Piano Sonatas. To learn the 32 works in the first place is a major feat for any pianist. But to perform the complete cycle in such a short time frame, with only 2 or 3 days between each concert, is a mammoth challenge that very few pianists would even contemplate let alone be able to rise to. To be able to walk on to the stage of the Royal Festival Hall – alone, no accompanist, no support, no music, just you and the piano – and play a total of more than eleven hours of music over eight separate evenings to 20,000 people is a skill given to very few. On so many levels it was a titanic achievement; a tremendous feat of musicianship, of intellect, of communication, of connection with an audience, not to mention the concentration, and technique, and memory that was involved. But Daniel Barenboim is a "born performer". The stage is where he is meant to be. This is his environment. He's like a "fish in water". He knows what he is here to do. And he believes in himself, believes that he can do it.

It goes without saying that any performer at any level needs self-belief. But great performers are masters of this. On the concert platform there can be no room for self-doubt: such thoughts have to remain well and truly in the practice studio. Daniel Barenboim was able to create such memorable evenings in the Royal Festival Hall because when he steps onto that stage he believes in himself completely. He knows the works as well as he possibly can and has done all the necessary study; he believes that he has something worth saying about the pieces, and has a view that is valid and worth sharing with people; and he believes that he is totally prepared and ready, both physically and mentally. Of course, he knows full well that at any moment the unexpected might happen. Maybe he'll be distracted by a member of the audience; or perhaps he'll lose concentration for a second or two – understandable when playing without the aid of the score for 11½ hours. Maybe he'll have a small memory slip. But if he does, he also believes and knows that he will be able to find a way through it and get back on track.

As Leaders in business it's really no different. Yes, over the years you have to have done all the study you can. And you've got to be physically and mentally prepared and ready. And you have to have developed your own unique take on the situation, so that people are in no doubt about who you are and what you stand for. But when the big moment arises – be it that Board meeting, or that client presentation, or a crucial interview – all humility and self-doubt have to be left in your equivalent of the "practice studio". It's time to believe in yourself.

So, my questions for you to reflect on are these:

Think of a team at work that you're a member of. What do you bring to that team that no-one else does?

Without being overly modest, what makes you unique? What makes you "YOU"? What is your greatest gift? When did you first realise you had this special talent?

Think of a time at work when you were at your best. What were you doing? What made your "performance" special? Which of your qualities were most evident?

What were the results? What was some of the feedback you received? How did you inspire others? How did that make you feel?

How do you maintain your craft? How could you bring even more of your special qualities to your work? What would the results be? How would that make you feel?

Think of a time outside of work when you were at your best. What were you doing? What made your "performance" special? Which of your gifts were most evident?

What were the results or effects on others? What was some of the feedback you received? How did that make you feel? How could you transfer those effects and results to your world of work?

Theme and Variations – Questioning

Theme –
The Experience of Questioning

"Ask an impertinent question and you are on the
way to the pertinent answer."

Jacob Bronowski

Back in the 1980s I lived in Hong Kong. It's a place where people take action, where things happen. They may not always be what you think should happen or be things that you like, but happen they do. The place never stays still. It's constantly being modified

It's not just the buildings and the skyline that are forever changing. It's the harbour itself. Because of the lack of flat ground – Hong Kong is mountainous – land reclamation has been a feature of the place for decades. I used to wonder why the home of The Royal HK Yacht Club was called Kellett Island, until I discovered that whilst the building is now surrounded by the high-rise of Causeway Bay, it was, back in the 1960s, a genuine island way out in the harbour.

This process of reclamation continues to this day. Getting off the Star Ferry in Central when I was last there, I realised that the pier was some distance from where I remembered it to have been 30 years earlier. A quick check on Google Maps revealed that the waterfront at Central is indeed now about a quarter-of-a-mile closer to Kowloon than it was just a few decades ago. The current Star Ferry piers are some 400 metres further out into the harbour than they were in my day.

Questions can move mountains

Given the premium on flat land, it's surprising that there is any space at all in Hong Kong for golf courses. But there are a few. And, while I was there, a new one was built on Lantau, the largest island that makes up Hong Kong. Lantau is the island where the International Airport is, and it's a bustling place. But back in the 1980s it was a backwater. Development was only just beginning, and one of the first centres was Discovery Bay, a new fledgling community popular with ex-pats. These purpose-built homes had almost everything you could want – space, peace and quiet, sea views, fast transport links to Central. They had everything … except a golf course! (We could discuss another time whether or not a golf course was really necessary! My real point is what happened next!). The problem with golf courses is that they need fairly level ground. And lots of it. And Lantau, like the rest of Hong Kong, is mountainous. It seemed impossible. But then someone posed the outrageous question: "If we were to chop the top off those hills and fill in these steep valleys with all the material, would that give us enough flat space on top to build a golf course?". Well, indeed it would. And sure enough, a few years later Discovery Bay Golf Club was opened.

Back in 2006, Eric Schmidt, the then CEO of Google famously said "We run the company by questions, not by answers." The act of asking questions – questions such as "What?" and "Why?", "Who?" and "Where?", "When?" and "How?" – is central to the lives of humans. As we've just seen, questions can almost literally "move mountains"! Questions are the driving force that move us forward. If we didn't question it's hard to imagine how we would ever be able to do anything.

And yet, there are plenty of organisations where questioning is not encouraged or rewarded. In fact, it's not even welcomed. Why might this be? Well, I said a few moments ago that asking questions is at the heart of our being. But could this very "central-ness" be a two-edged sword, be part of the problem? Maybe we take asking questions for granted and underestimate their power? Maybe, at some level, we associate questions with childhood: after all, who hasn't been irritated by a 5-year old repeatedly asking "Why?"! Maybe we see "asking questions" as something we should grow out of as we get older. Or perhaps we view questioning as a commonplace, something that even children can do, and therefore of little worth?

And, if questions are often not appreciated in our work lives, what about our home lives? How many of us question things as a matter of course? We probably know that we should, but when things become difficult, do we always look for new ways, or do we tend to simply plough on, carrying on doing what we've always done. In our frantic 21st century lives, how many of us have the time to question what we are doing and where we are going? Or, perhaps more to the point, how many of us have the courage to ask ourselves the profound questions?

Asking creates "buy-in"

Countless times a day we pose questions of others and ourselves. Questions are the basis of conversation. They help us create a dialogue, as opposed to a monologue. Just take a moment to consider how many times a day on the phone or face-to-face you ask somebody "How are you?" or "How are you doing?". Perhaps you then move on to … "What was the traffic like this morning?" … "What are you having for lunch?" … "Where are you going on holiday?". Of course, questions at this level are mundane in the extreme, but they have their use, "oiling the wheels" of relationship.

The beauty of questions is that they engage us. We cannot ignore them. They hold us and force us to be involved, in the way that statements simply don't. I guess we've all sat through presentations or talks, where we've been "lectured to" for half-an-hour or more. And, let's be honest, didn't your mind wander? The subject matter might well have been rather good, but "statements", and "lectures", and being "talked at" make us passive. Being "told things" lets us switch off and disengage, whereas "asking us" draws us in and causes us to think and be creative. And when that creativity enables us to come up with an answer – OUR answer – then we are far more likely to follow through and take action, more so than if we'd been told what to do by someone else. Asking people creates "buy-in".

Questions are also important because they change the very nature of relationships. When someone is in "telling" mode, there is an implication that they are the expert: they know something that the other person doesn't. There is an implied hierarchy: they are superior, the other is inferior. Or – perhaps in terms of Transactional Analysis – they are the Parent, the other is the Child. But these relationships change when you ask questions. When you ask others for their ideas, when you take your team seriously, when you make time to seek their views, it can be truly empowering. It's perhaps the quickest way to give others confidence and help them develop a sense of responsibility. When you ask rather than tell, then your colleagues automatically become peers rather than subordinates. Questions have a way of showing respect and demonstrating to people that you value them and see them as equals. And with this approach comes trust and transparency.

So, my questions for you to reflect on are these:

When have you consciously used an "asking" style with colleagues?
What was going on? What effect did it have?

Why did you choose that approach? What were you hoping to achieve?
What did you achieve? How great was the temptation to "tell"?
What might have happened if you had?

When have you ever "switched off" during a presentation? Why was it?
What was it about the speaker's style?

How could the speaker have engaged you more? What might the outcome have been? How can you make sure your presentations engage people?

If Google "run the company by questions, not by answers" what would be the benefit to your organisation of doing the same? What steps could you take to make this happen?

How do you encourage questions in your team? How do you ensure that questions are welcomed and then rewarded?

When have you had a "Discovery Bay Golf Club" moment and asked yourself an outrageous question? What impossibility were you facing? What was the outcome?

When have you been coached to discover "your answer" to a problem? How did you follow through and take action? What did you feel like?

When have you been given an answer and told to take action on it? What did you feel like? How can you make sure this never happens in your team?

Variation 1 –
Questioning whether things matter

"Questions draw us together.
Answers push us apart."

Peter Block

The American author, Peter Block, is most known for his best-selling books, Flawless Consulting, The Empowered Manager, and Stewardship. My favourite of his works, however, is the small volume, enigmatically titled "The Answer to How is Yes". In it he describes the way that we, as a society, have become increasingly efficient. He shows how astonishingly good we are at achieving and doing ever more things. And yet, at the same time, so many of these things that we achieve have little value, over time they mean less and less. The title of the book points to our culture's worship of a "how-to" mentality. We crave answers. And, so, we seek advice from others, we attend workshops, we read books, we study for additional qualifications, we gain more skills. We habitually ask "How?". But if our aim is actually "Acting on what matters" – which, incidentally, is the book's tag-line – he suggests that we would be better off if we started by asking ourselves "Why?" rather than "How?".

It's tempting to believe that asking "How?" – or indeed similar questions such as "When?", "Who?", "What?" – get us closer to the answer. But, paradoxically, such questions often take us further away. For a start, the question "How?" implies that there is a solution to be found. This might be far from the truth. Just because you can ask a question doesn't mean that there is automatically an answer. Asking "How?" also reinforces the belief that life is primarily utilitarian, that it's about getting things done, that it's about producing and achieving. So often in organisations, time spent not doing these things is seen to have been squandered. But what about the time we spend thinking, discussing, reflecting, imagining, listening, mulling things over, creating? Is that time wasted? Of course not. It's actually essential.

For Peter Block, it's not that asking "How?" is wrong, per se. It's that "How?" is rarely the most important question, and so should be asked later rather than sooner. But we live in an urgent society. We're invariably so desperate to get things done, to get going, to take action, to do something – ANYTHING! – that in the process we often fail to check whether it's the right action.

We also blind ourselves to the fact that we almost certainly know the answers already. Asking "How?" presupposes that we don't yet know what to do. But ask any Coach and they will tell you tales of clients who knew "the answer" to their problems right from Day 1. They already knew what the best course of action was. All they needed from the Coach was help in articulating it.

The question "How?" comes very much from our left hemisphere. It's a desire to find control and certainty in a world which we so often experience as uncertain and chaotic. We find consolation in a belief that there is a "right way", that there is a solution, and that we can find out what it is. But even if we do find a solution and act on it, there is no guarantee that we will be "acting on what matters". After all, when we say something matters, we must be clear about to whom it matters. Our work may "matter" to others – for example, our results and achievements might matter to our manager, or to our CEO, or to the shareholders – but does our work matter to us?

The wrong question? The wrong time?

As I've mentioned above, Peter Block isn't saying that "How?"-type questions are wrong in themselves. It's rather that we need to delay their use. He suggests we be less eager to ask certain questions, in particular, these six:

- How do you do it?
- How long will it take?
- How much does it cost?
- How do you get those people to change?
- How do we measure it?
- How have other people done it successfully?

How do you do it?

This is the most simple and plain variety of the "How?" questions. The vanilla version. Although it suggests, erroneously, that you don't know the answer, nevertheless it does imply that there is an answer within reach and that it is straightforward. And that is very appealing. Of course, if only we gave it a moment's thought we would recognise that answers to life's important questions are never straightforward. And that's because life is complex, life is full of paradox.

Rather than avoiding the complexity of life, perhaps we should embrace it. Rather than sidestepping the profound questions maybe we should learn to approach them "as a philosopher instead of an engineer."

How long will it take?

In a world where we celebrate speed – think Usain Bolt, Formula 1, the Olympics – and a world where we want everything immediately – think downloading and streaming, Amazon, Uber, Deliveroo – it's no surprise that the question "How long?" seems so important.

We trick ourselves into believing that our focus on "speed" will make change happen more quickly, despite all the data which points to the contrary. We prefer "Now" to "Later", even if we're aware that "Later" might give a better result, a more sustainable result. We go for the "quick fix" even though evidence shows that it won't last.

What we have to learn is that profound change happens at the speed that it happens. It can't be rushed. "How long will it take?", therefore, is one of those questions that has no answer.

How much does it cost?

One of the themes of Iain McGilchrist's book, "The Master and his Emissary", is that there are aspects of our lives which, important as they are, should never control us. They are, if you like, great "servants" but must never become "The Master". The world of finance is one such element. It is crucial to our lives. We can't run a modern society without it. But there is clearly a huge danger if it takes over and we come to see everything through a financial lens. Yes, we all want "value for money". Yes, we might all "shop around" occasionally for better deals on our groceries. But would any of us, if we needed brain surgery, choose our surgeon because they were cheap or were offering a "Buy-One-Get-One-Free" promotion?

Although we try to monetise everything and put a value on "people" and "the environment" and "safety" and "justice" – ie: things that matter – we all know that it's smoke and mirrors. Such things are beyond value. When we ask "How much does it cost?" what we're really asking is "Is it cheap?". But, unfortunately, "Acting on what matters" can never be cheap.

How do you get those people to change?

I mentioned above that "How?" questions satisfy the left hemisphere's need for control. Well, this question is all about control and power and authority over others. Whether it's about controlling our children or our spouses or our colleagues or our clients, one thing for sure is that it's almost always about them, and never about us. We don't need to change, they do. Of course, we dress things up by saying "We want to help them". But, actually, we want to control them, because when we focus on others we're able to deflect attention from ourselves.

How do we measure it?

The implication here is that "If you can't measure it then it doesn't exist". Once again, as with "How long?" and "How much?", the question itself is not wrong. The act of measurement has its place. Through technological advances measurement has improved our lives and helped us in so many different ways. And yet, we all know that what really gives life value – what "matters" – can never be measured. There is no way, and never will be, of calibrating qualities such as Love or Care, Beauty or Passion, Friendship or Humour.

How have other people done it successfully?

Once again, the left hemisphere's need for control underpins this question. There is a desire for certainty where none can ever exist. There is a hope that by discovering how something worked in Situation X that it will be possible to transfer it risk-free to Situation Y. But this can never happen, because as we've seen several times thus far, the world is forever changing and every situation is unique. Much as we would like to have them, there are no road maps for us to follow in the real world. We're on our own. As Peter Block comments "The value of another's experience is to give us hope, not to tell us how or whether to proceed."

So, my questions for you to reflect on are these:

When have you asked a "How?" question too early? What would have happened if you'd asked "Why?" instead? What might the benefits have been?

What might the benefits be of sometimes approaching life "as a philosopher instead of an engineer"?

When has a focus on "speed" – going for the "quick fix" – ever backfired? What would have been the better option?

Regarding "cost", when has seeking the "cheaper option" worked for you? When has it not? What have you learned?

Instead of asking "How can I get people to change?", what changes might need to happen in you?

When you think of "What matters", what measurements might be possible? What would have meaning for you?

When you've asked how others have accomplished something, what have you learned? In what ways has asking the question helped you?

When you think of "Acting on what matters", what matters to your boss, to your organisation, to your colleagues, to your direct reports? What do they want from you?

Which of these things really matter to you? What else matters to you?

Variation 2 –
Questioning what does matter

"It is better to know some of the questions
than all of the answers."

James Thurber

I mentioned earlier that part of the power of questions is that they engage us. We can't disregard them. They draw us in and then they hold us and force us to be involved, in the way that statements simply don't.

We've just looked at six "How?" questions that Peter Block recommends we delay asking, questions that should be posed later rather than sooner. Well now we're going to examine six more questions, but this time they're ones that should be raised sooner rather than later! And that's because they're designed to help you explore what matters to you. The six questions are:

- What refusal have you been postponing?
- What commitment are you prepared to make?
- What is the price you are willing to pay?
- What is your contribution to the problem you are concerned with?
- What is the crossroad at which you find yourself in your life?
- What do you want to create together?

What refusal have you been postponing?

Central to Carl Jung's work was the concept of "a tension of opposites, without which no forward movement is possible". He talked of polarities such as the Conscious and the Unconscious, Introversion and Extraversion, Thinking and Feeling, Sensation and Intuition. The idea is that you can't have one without the other.

Both concepts shape each other and give each other meaning. The same goes for physical entities such as mountain peaks and valleys, as well as intangibles such as hot and cold, and wet and dry.

It also applies to Yes and No. Without the opposite neither word has any meaning, neither has value. In my workshops I am forever hearing over-worked people confess "I just can't say No." Whether it's as a result of fear or a desire to please, at some level, they have a belief that they must always say "Yes", that they must agree to every demand made of them. But then they explain that their strategy doesn't work, that they're not appreciated, and instead are taken for granted by their boss and their colleagues. Well, of course they are! Their "Yes" is worthless. As Peter Block points out "If we cannot say no, then our yes means nothing."

What commitment are you prepared to make?

Achieving anything worthwhile takes an inordinate amount of effort. Malcolm Gladwell, in his book "Outliers", suggests that 10,000 hours of practice is the minimum needed to have any chance of reaching a level of mastery. This might sound a lot, but certainly in the world of classical music the figures seem to stack up. Concert pianists whom we might see playing with major orchestras will all have started their studies at the age of 5 or 6, some even earlier. For the first few years they may have practised only 2 or 3 hours a day but by the time they reached the age of 10 or so, many will have ramped that up to 5 or 6 hours. So by their mid/late-teens they will all have hit the 10,000 hour mark, and then some.

This is an astonishing level of commitment, especially when you consider that there are no guarantees. For every pianist that we see walking onto the stage of the Royal Festival Hall, there will be another hundred, maybe a thousand, who will never play there despite the fact that they, too, have clocked up their 10,000 hours of practice. Such people put the work in not because someone – their boss, their parents, "society" – says they should, but because they want to, because they choose to. Because it matters. Because they're committed.

What is the price you are willing to pay?

2018 saw the release of the film, Free Solo, which profiles rock climber, Alex Honnold, on his quest to perform a free solo climb of El Capitan in June 2017. For those who are not particularly familiar with the world of climbing, El Capitan is a 3200ft sheer granite wall in Yosemite National Park in California. It was first climbed in the 1950s, and since then has been on the To-do list of every serious rock climber. Alex Honnold has climbed it many times and holds several records. What made his climb in June 2017 special was that it was the very first "free solo" ascent of "El Cap", as it's affectionately known. What this means is that he climbed without using ropes. He went up this 3200ft vertical face using no safety gear whatsoever. The only connection he had to the rock was his finger tips and his shoes. Apart from these, he was completely unattached.

The consequences of this are very simple. He knows that if he makes a single mistake he will die. There are no ifs and buts. There is no safety net, actual or metaphorical. If he loses concentration for a moment he will fall. And that is the end. There is no "Take 2".

Why would anyone take such risks? Why would they put themselves on the line, their life on the line? Because in that moment they are fully ALIVE. They are doing what matters, even if the price is extreme.

What is your contribution to the problem you're concerned with?

In recent years, to try and understand what happened during the 2008 financial crash I've become particularly interested in Economics and the global economic system. There was a question I became obsessed by: "How and why did we construct a financial system that is both so sophisticated and yet, at the same time, so fragile that it could pretty much collapse?" As a result of my studies – reading countless books, articles and blogs – I now have a much better grasp of the subject. I can speak the language of finance and banking with a modicum of fluency, and I can see how such a system was created.

Initially, I, like many others, put the blame for the crash fairly and squarely on "The Bankers", a conveniently anonymous group that we could all rail against. I would also be happy to condemn "The Government", though quite which government I was condemning wasn't always clear. I would explain to anyone that would listen how the seeds of the 2008 crash were sown way back in the 1970s – Neoliberalism, Thatcherism, Reaganomics.

All of which might be true. But it then occurred to me that, by coincidence, my own career started in the 1970s. I have been a working, voting, tax-paying adult and citizen for the whole of this 30+ year period. So, this God-awful mess that kicked off in 2008 and is still going on, it happened on "my watch". It's MY fault. OK, not mine entirely, but my generation is to blame. It's not the fault of my children's generation or my parents'. It's my generation. We didn't do anything to stop it. Of course, I can offer plenty of reasons why we did nothing – ignorance, trust in authority, busy being parents… blah, blah, blah. But they're all excuses.

The point is that for decades we chose to blame someone else. We didn't choose accountability. We preferred to be in the audience rather than on stage, to be spectators rather than players. We chose not to act on what matters. And now we have no-one to blame but ourselves.

What is the crossroad at which you find yourself at this point in your life?

In July 1969 I was there in front of the TV when Neil Armstrong and Buzz Aldrin took the very first steps on the moon. The whole Apollo 11 mission, from blast off at Cape Kennedy to splash-down in the

Pacific was just eight days, but that week changed the astronauts' lives forever. Both Armstrong and Aldrin had been fighter pilots in the Korean War, and then test pilots, before joining NASA. In July 1969 they were aged 38 and 39 respectively. They were both reaching their prime. And yet after that week spent going to the moon their flying days were behind them.

I remember, as a teenager, wondering "What do they do next? How do you follow a trip to the moon? What else can ever match that achievement?". As it turned out, these were reasonable questions to ask. Many astronauts, Buzz Aldrin in particular, had great difficulties when they found themselves at the Post-NASA Crossroads. But it's not just astronauts that can suffer. Everyone one of us can and will lose our way at some point. High points in life are fleeting. Nobody can and does stay at the top of Everest for long. After fifteen minutes, it's always time to head back down to "the real world". And then we all need to regroup and decide "What next? Which direction do I go in? What do I want to pursue? What matters?"

What do you want to create together?

At its worst, organisational life can be dispiriting. It can result in people feeling a lack of belonging and involvement, as well as them having little direction and purpose. "I'm just a cog in a machine" is a phrase we've probably all heard someone say.

But the act of creation, and in particular being given the power to choose what we want to create, can reverse all that negativity. When we give life to an idea, when we develop and nurture a concept that originated in our imagination, we become an artist. We suddenly know what it is to create.

But we can go further. We can create together. It's been said that Life is a team sport. Although we like to think that we are independent and separate and individual, this is actually an illusion. We live in an inter-dependent world and rely on others almost totally for our survival. We depend on countless people around us – colleagues, associates, team-mates, friends, family members, partners – for support and our well-being. But we also depend on those that have gone before us, those that have helped create the societal infrastructure that supports us. As Sir Isaac Newton observed, we're all "standing on ye shoulders of Giants." Staying with the Himalayan theme for a moment longer, no-one climbs Everest by themselves. Yes, I know that there have been one or two Sherpas that have solo-ed from Base-camp to the summit, climbing the "last" 11,000ft in a matter of hours, but even they needed plenty of support to get themselves and their equipment to Base-camp. They've all relied on a large team who helped them get to the top.

So, my questions for you to reflect on are simple and straightforward:

What refusal have you been postponing?

What commitment are you prepared to make?

What is the price you are willing to pay?

What is your contribution to the problem you're concerned with?

What is the crossroad at which you find yourself at this point in your life?

What do you want to create together?

Variation 3 –
Questioning our freedom

> "It is difficult to free fools
> from the chains they revere."
>
> *Voltaire (attrib)*

Have you ever wondered how to train Fleas? I guess probably not. But if you ever do there is a great little video on YouTube that's worth checking out. It shows a scene in a science laboratory and a guy in a white lab coat. The rather humourless voice-over explains "Training fleas requires a glass jar and a lid. The fleas are placed inside the jar and the lid is then sealed. They are left undisturbed for three days. Then, when the jar is opened the fleas will not jump out. In fact, the fleas will never jump higher than the level set by the lid. Their behaviour is now set for the rest of their lives. And when these fleas reproduce their offspring will automatically follow their example." After a reflective pause, the video ends with the words "Escape the circus and live beyond the limits of the imaginary lid".

We've previously examined questions that might help us establish what does not and what does matter in our lives. But why is this even an issue? Why don't we already know what's important for us? And why don't we act on it?

By the way – I realise that the Flea video may be fake. Perhaps it's all done with CGI. I don't know, and it doesn't matter. It's only a metaphor. The point is that we put limits on ourselves. And these limits – the "imaginary lid" – are many and varied. Authority, Evidence, Touchy-feely stuff, Security, Not being ready. We might have hidden behind them all at some point.

Authority

We've all heard office banter along the lines of "Oh, that's well above my pay grade"…"It's not my job, guv"…"It's not my circus, not my monkeys". These quips speak to a powerlessness that we can easily feel, a belief that our destiny is in somebody else's hands, that the reasons for our lack of freedom lie with someone else – our manager, the Exec team, the Board, the Organisation, the Government, "Brussels!" – rather than with ourselves.

The flippant remarks also imply a lack of connection and involvement. We forget that the organisation is us, the Exec Team represents us, the Government represents us. As Peter Block comments, "We complain about the culture as if we were only visitors here." But you're not a visitor. You're not just passing through. This is it. This world is yours. This is the world that you have helped to create. If you feel disengaged it's probably because you're not doing what matters to you. When things do matter it's hard to be detached.

Evidence

Spending time on "Due Diligence" can be important. But mostly it's limiting. When we're dealing with human systems not only is history notoriously bad at predicting what's in store for us – after all, we're not machines and so the past does not equal the future – but it will also only ever tell you about somebody else's experience. Research can never tell you about what you will experience, because you are different, your situation is different, your time is different.

But, hey, let's look on the bright side! That unnecessary piece of evidence that you've just discovered, those redundant facts, that needless audit, they're all a great way of procrastinating and delaying taking action on what truly matters. So, it wasn't all wasted!

Touchy-feely stuff

My work is about helping people "look in the mirror". The idea is a simple one: before you can understand and connect better with others – your colleagues, your team, your boss, your clients – you need to understand you … your behaviours, reactions, drives, motivations. Some refer to this as Emotional Intelligence. Others, more disparagingly, describe it as "touchy-feely bollocks".

Over the years I've worked with delegates – sadly, too many of them – that believed that there is no room in the workplace for emotion or anything personal. For them, work is about rationality, analysis, logic. My view is that work is indeed about those things. But it's also about a whole lot more. It's about what matters to you.

The more of yourself that you bring to the table the better off you'll be and the better the result. If you only bring the "logical you" and leave the "emotional you" back at home, it's like getting into a boxing ring with one hand tied behind your back. Good Luck if you think that will bring you success!

Security

Back in 2014, Simon Sinek gave a TEDtalk entitled "Why Good Leaders Make You Feel Safe". The fact that it's been viewed more than 10 million times suggests that it speaks to people, that it resonates with them. In a volatile, uncertain, complex, ambiguous world we all want to feel safe. And so we latch on to and follow those who can help us, those who will protect us. But as with all aspects of life there is a trade-off. The price of that safety is our freedom.

Life entails risk. Pursuing what matters entails risk. Neither of these sit well with a desire for certainty and safety.

Not being ready

We all know that "the right time" is a fiction. It doesn't exist. If you wait for the "right time" to get married, to have a family, to start a business, to move to the countryside, to take up Yoga … then you'll be waiting forever. We fool ourselves into believing that we don't have enough of whatever it is that we think we need. We convince ourselves that we don't have enough money, enough experience, enough education, enough skills, enough practice. We believe that we don't have enough. And we also believe that we are not enough.

We don't trust ourselves. And as a result we postpone living. We postpone being "alive" until another day, until tomorrow. But, as the saying goes, "There are only so many tomorrows."

So, my questions for you to reflect on are these:

What are some of the imaginary lids that have restricted your ability to jump?

When have you hidden behind "authority"? What was going on for you? What else could you have done?

When have you overdone your Due Diligence? What happened? What was the effect? What did you miss out on?

How easy is it for you to bring ALL aspects of you to the table? What are the benefits? What do your colleagues gain? What do you gain?

What is your relationship with risk? How much security do you need? How much safety are you prepared to lose in order to gain freedom?

When have you waited for the "right time" to do something? Did that time ever arrive? When have you trusted yourself and admitted "I'm ready!"

Variation 4 –
Questioning our speed

"If you want to improve how you manage time –
stop doing what doesn't need to be done!"

Peter Drucker

My old car didn't have SatNav. I was OK with that. (Well, mostly I was). I liked to think that I have a pretty good sense of direction and so, once I'd looked at a map, I was confident that I knew where I was going. Needless to say this confidence was sometimes misplaced. Yes, unaided, I could usually get myself fairly close to where I was going – perhaps to within a mile or two – but then that's when the fun started. Often, late at night, I found myself in some rural backwater, circling a Marriott Hotel, but it was nowhere to be seen. I was up and down featureless country lanes searching in vain for any clues.

But here's the interesting thing: What I found was that, as time moved on and it got later and later, I would start to drive more quickly. I was lost. And I was feeling anxious. And the effect on me was that I put my foot down on the accelerator.

But why? Why do we speed up when we're lost? Ten minutes earlier, when I knew where I was going, I was happy to cruise along. But now, disoriented and uncertain of the route, I put my foot down! This is bizarre behaviour. If I'm unsure of where I'm going, if I think I'm heading towards the wrong place, what on earth is the point of getting there faster? It's not logical. Of course, it isn't. But there seems to be a weird connection between increased speed and confusion. The more perplexed and bewildered we are, the faster we tend to go.

By contrast, we've all heard anecdotes about people experiencing "time almost standing still". At moments of extreme intensity and focus and importance, our perceptions seem to change. Those involved in a car accident often report being able to recall every detail in slow motion, even though the whole event lasted just a few seconds. In professional sport we hear similar claims, when a cricket batsman describes having "all the time in the world", even though the ball they're facing is approaching them at 100 mph or more.

Time dilation is also a common experience in warfare. Ant Middleton, the ex-Special Forces soldier, describes it this way: "Going into an operation – the moment I made contact with the enemy – I'd enter a completely different psychological space. Your brain goes into a hyper-efficient state, absorbing so much information from your surroundings that it really does feel as if the clock has suddenly slowed down – as if you've got the ability to control time itself."

The common denominator here, the thing which perhaps connects these three scenarios – the car accident, elite sport, the military engagement with the enemy – is that for those involved "it matters". In fact, in those fleeting moments – moments of total focus and purpose – nothing else matters. And that is when we find that "we have time".

Could this be saying something about our 21st century way of life? Might our current fetish for speed be symptomatic of a deeper disorientation and panic? Why do we feel the need to drive flat out all the time, to have diaries that are full, to be constantly occupied? When I chat to clients and ask "How are you?", the most common response is along the lines of "Oh. Very busy. We're frantic here!". They might then add, perhaps to reassure themselves "…but it's good. There's lots going on". But nobody has ever replied "It's fabulous. Work is great. The balance is just right. I've got enough to do, but, more importantly, I also have time to think and reflect on what I'm doing, on what we're doing." Nobody has ever said that to me.

I am also intrigued when the tables are turned and someone else initiates the conversation with me. Invariably colleagues will start with "Hi Charles, how are you doing? Are you busy?" – the assumption being that "busy-ness" is the only positive way to be. But why is it good to be busy, to never switch off? Why is it good to be connected "virtually" 24/7? ... and yet, at the same time, have little space for meaningful face-to-face connection? Why is it good to reply to every email immediately? ... to answer messages at the weekend and on holiday? Why is it good to lack time for reflection and thought? ... to avoid the time necessary for depth? We live in a superficial world of Twitter and sound-bites. The BBC News website even boasts a page entitled "In a hurry? Here's what you need to know in five minutes".

Why have we chosen Quantity rather than Quality? How have we come to accept "Virtual meetings" ... "Online learning" ... "Fast food"? ... even "Virtual sex with avatars" (According to today's BBC 'In a hurry?' page, this is what the year 2039 has in store for us!). Why do we tolerate these "signs of progress" when they're so obviously inferior to the "real thing"?

The common refrain is that "We don't have time". And, you're right: you don't have time to do everything. You most certainly don't have time to do all the crap. But here's the thing. There is always time, and I mean always time to do what is important, to do what matters. In fact, if there isn't time for something then it's a sure sign that it probably doesn't matter.

So, my questions for you to reflect on are these:

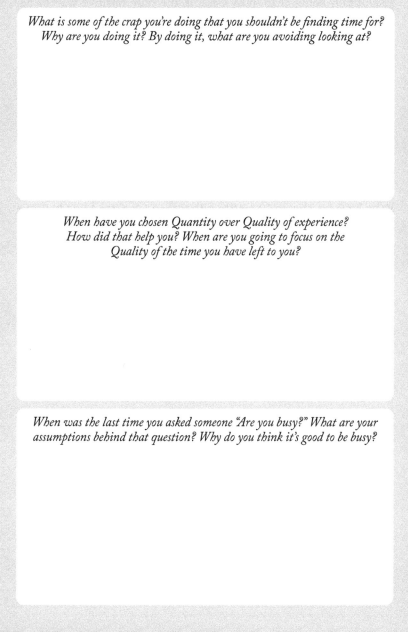

What is some of the crap you're doing that you shouldn't be finding time for? Why are you doing it? By doing it, what are you avoiding looking at?

When have you chosen Quantity over Quality of experience? How did that help you? When are you going to focus on the Quality of the time you have left to you?

When was the last time you asked someone "Are you busy?" What are your assumptions behind that question? Why do you think it's good to be busy?

How does being busy help you? How does it get in your way?

When did you last disconnect completely from the online world – ie: switch off your phone/laptop/PC – and spend time simply with the people around you? How long did you switch off for? What was good about it?

When have you experienced "time almost standing still"? What was going on for you? What was important about it? Why did it matter?

Variation 5 –
Questioning appreciatively

"Ask what's possible, not what's wrong.
Keep asking."

Margaret J. Wheatley

Back in the 1980s, when David Cooperrider was working on his Doctoral thesis, he did some initial analysis on what had been written in the field of Organisational Development. He wanted to assess current trends and thinking amongst the academic community and so he trawled through thousands of research papers. What was particularly enlightening was not so much the details of the individual papers, but rather the approach taken by the vast majority of authors of all of these studies. What most struck Cooperrider was that more than 90% of all the studies started from a negative standpoint, from a perspective of deficiency. In almost every study, the team in question – or the department, or the organisation as a whole – were being judged as if they were in some way dysfunctional. There was almost an assumption that they were damaged or defective; that things were broken, not working properly, and had to be mended; that something was missing and therefore ought to be replaced.

Now, the cynics amongst you might be thinking "90% seems low to me. 100% of the teams I've ever worked in have been dysfunctional!". But, joking aside, is that really likely? I'm no statistician, but I'd have guessed some sort of Bell Curve/Normal distribution would be at play here. Common sense – plus my experience of working with 100s of groups – suggests that in the workplace there's a handful of teams that we might describe as "High Performing", another handful at the opposite end of the spectrum which we could call "Wholly Wretched", and a large majority in the middle where things are "Good Enough", where behaviours could definitely be better but where they certainly don't warrant perjorative adjectives such as "dysfunctional" or "defective".

Words create worlds

I believe in the maxim We see what we want to see. If I was to go into an organisation – let's say, your organisation – what I would find will depend almost entirely on what I look for, on the questions I ask, on the words I use. There is no "one" view of the organisation waiting, objectively, to be discovered by me. There are multiple views, as many (and, actually, more) as there are people in the organisation. And they're all subjective. However much we might try to be objective and see "what is", our interactions will inevitably be subjective ones. It cannot be otherwise. We construct the world that we inhabit. As Joseph Jaworski has written, "I had always thought that we used language to describe the world. Now I see that it is through language that we create the world. We do not describe the world we see. We see the world we describe."

So, let's imagine I spend time in your organisation. And then let's further imagine that I decide to ignore any good qualities you and your colleagues might have and, instead, I focus on the negatives, what needs to be better. So, in a workshop I announce: "OK. So that we can start to improve things around here, I want you all to tell me about examples of poor communication, weak leadership, shoddy teamwork, inadequate support from your colleagues, lousy customer service". Well, if I ask those sorts of questions then I'm pretty sure that people would come up with examples. It may take a while to tease them out, but those things exist everywhere. They may not be immediately obvious, but they are there. It's just what life is like. If you look for dysfunction then you will find it.

On the other hand, let's imagine I chose to start the workshop with a slightly different inquiry? What if changed the words I used and focused on the positives? What if I opened with "OK. So that we can make things even better around here I first want to hear of examples of fabulous communication, inspiring leadership, outstanding teamwork, great support from your colleagues, exemplary customer service. Then we're going to explore ways of building on these examples". Well, I will find those too. Again, it may take a while to tease them all out, but they are there. In the very same team. Because such positive qualities exist everywhere, in every team, regardless of how "high performing" or how "wretched" they may seem. Once again, you find what you look for.

Accentuate the positive

In 1944 Johnny Mercer and Harold Arlen provided the score for the film "Here Come the WAVES". A wartime romantic comedy, it starred Bing Crosby and Betty Hutton, and featured a number that was later to be nominated for the Academy Award for Best Original Song. According to the lyrics…

> You've got to accentuate the positive
> Eliminate the negative
> Latch on to the affirmative
> Don't mess with Mister In-Between

The song is in the style of a sermon – it was inspired by the African American preacher, Father Divine – and explains that accentuating the positive is the key to happiness. It's a simple message, but one repeatedly ignored by organisations.

Unfortunately, it's all too common for organisations to concentrate on negatives, on problems, on what's not working, on why things go wrong, on who isn't up-to-speed. And soon the workplace is filled with unhappiness, with demoralising stories of failure. Those who dare to challenge this tone are often branded as being "unrealistic" … "not in the real world" … "naïve" … "dreamers" … "blue sky thinkers".

David Cooperrider's PhD laid the foundation for what has since come to be known as Appreciative Inquiry, an approach to Organisational change rooted very firmly in being positive, being affirmative, concentrating on possibilities rather than problems. Many traditional OD models take a deficit approach to analysis – they look at threats, barriers, causes of failure, resistance, gaps. Cooperrider's instinct was to examine the organisation when it's working at its very best – not only what's good about it now, but also how great it's been in the past, and how great it could be in the future.

Imagine without limits

The point I want to stress in all of this is "Which type of questions are more likely to lead to positive outcomes and positive change?" It's not that problems are unimportant. They certainly are, and they need to be acknowledged, not ignored. But when we ask negative questions – What's gone wrong? What's not working? What's failing? What's broken? – there is an underlying assumption that what we're trying and hoping to do is get back to "where we were" before the failure. It's as if we're saying – "Something has gone wrong ... We're now flat on our backs ... How can we get back to where we were, say, six months ago". The trouble with this method is that we're immediately limiting ourselves to what's happened in the past. It presupposes that "where we were" is worth getting back to. But maybe "where we were" wasn't that great, and is not worth getting back to. Could this be the opportunity we've been looking for to set our sights higher, to chase our collective dreams?

When you ask positive questions – ones such as "What's already working well here? What are your successes? Can you describe examples of great teamwork, communication, influence, client support, leadership? What was the focus in those instances? Can they be replicated?" – the assumption is different. It's a belief that there are limitless possibilities. This time, it's as if we're saying "Despite the problem, we're still functioning ... Yes, there are challenges but that's OK … What are all the things we are absolutely fabulous at? … How can we make the most of these and become great?"

When we approach setbacks in this way, participants are far more positive and creative when exploring future possibilities for themselves and the team. The benefits of this mindset are obvious. It encourages people to imagine without limits.

So, my questions for you to reflect on are these:

> *When did you last "imagine without limits"? What was going on for you? How did it make you feel?*

> *When you ask yourself some of the above positive questions, what are your answers? How excited do they make you feel?*

> *Who would you describe as being "unrealistic, not-in-the-real-world, naïve, a dreamer"? Why? What might they have to offer you?*

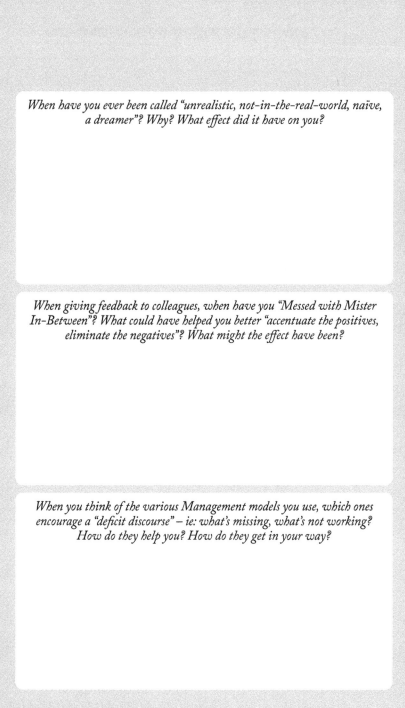

When have you ever been called "unrealistic, not-in-the-real-world, naïve, a dreamer"? Why? What effect did it have on you?

When giving feedback to colleagues, when have you "Messed with Mister In-Between"? What could have helped you better "accentuate the positives, eliminate the negatives"? What might the effect have been?

When you think of the various Management models you use, which ones encourage a "deficit discourse" – ie: what's missing, what's not working? How do they help you? How do they get in your way?

Variation 6 –
Questioning psychologically

"Archetypes resemble the beds of rivers:
dried up because the water has deserted them,
though it may return at any time.
An archetype is something like an old
watercourse along which the water of life flowed
for a time, digging a deep channel for itself.
The longer it flowed the deeper the channel,
and the more likely it is that sooner or later
the water will return."

Carl Jung

According to the most recent UN estimate, the current population of the world is c.7.7 billion. And of course, we're all different! There will never be another "you". Every one of us is unique.

And yet, for all this diversity in how we look and sound and behave and what we experience, we're all "human". There is so much that we all share, so much that connects us across the divisions of race and colour and beliefs.

When we ask ourselves "Who am I?"– the most fundamental question we can ever ask ourselves – I guess we're trying to understand these two things: What makes us different from everyone else and What makes us similar? What separates us and what binds us together? And it's at this point that many people turn to the psychologist, Carl Jung, for guidance because he spent a lifetime considering these questions, exploring both the "universal" and the "particular". As we have seen in an earlier essay, his work on Psychological Types looked at the "individual", and examined how we differ in our ways of experiencing the world around us – ie: what makes us unique. When it comes to what connects us and what we share, Jung employed the concept of the "Collective Unconscious" – an "archaic heritage of humanity"– which he believed to be made up of certain functional units called "archetypes".

In Physics and Chemistry, the belief that matter is made up of discrete units is a very old idea. To begin with, the smallest particle was thought to be the atom – in fact, the word comes from the Greek word atomos meaning "uncuttable". But then it was discovered that atoms were indeed "cuttable" into even smaller bits and pieces, and these then became known as protons and neutrons and electrons. For a while, these were all believed to be "elementary", but as time has gone on this picture, too, has changed. As it now stands, the set of particles said today to be elementary is known as the Standard Model, and it includes the exotic sounding quarks, bosons and leptons.

The idea of there being a set of basic building blocks can also be seen in biology. The whole field of genetics is based on the existence of discrete inheritable units – genes – an idea first suggested by Gregor Mendel in the 1860s. Although he did not coin the term gene, he explained how these individual units give rise to inherited visible physical characteristics.

In the way that biologists investigate genes, and physicists research waves and particles, Jung believed that it was the business of psychologists to study archetypes – the basic elements that he thought compose the collective unconscious.

An archetype is a way of thinking, an image, that all members of a culture experience. The customary example given of an archetype is that of the "Mother". It's a universal image, and one that we all recognise. And at the same time, we all have an individual connection and relationship with the word through having a mother of our own.

Archetypes, then, are a collection of a whole range of possibilities and qualities that can help us understand ourselves and our place within the world that we've created. There are countless archetypes, but for the purposes of this essay I'm going to take a look at just four. By drawing again on the writings of Peter Block, I want to explore briefly the worlds of the Engineer, the Economist, the Artist, and the Architect. Hopefully these different perspectives can shine a light on one or two aspects of our culture.

The Engineer

The world of the archetypal "Engineer" is one that is tangible and real and mechanical. The engineer enjoys discovering how things work – getting to understand the underlying theory – and so is fascinated by processes and systems. As a result, the engineer speaks the languages of maths and physics fluently.

Engineers like to measure and predict and be in control of their world, to be on top of things at all times, to avoid surprises. They appreciate the predictability of machines, the fact that, by and large, machines do what you expect them to do. An engineer finds it reassuring that pieces of engineering work in a very linear "cause and effect" manner – you turn the control to the left or right and something definable happens: you press this lever and that happens. It might be complicated but at the same time it's all very understandable.

Engineers also derive comfort from the fact that machines are extremely reliable and safe. One reason is that there are rules to be followed. To some people, rules are off-putting and restricting, but for an engineer rules provide boundaries to what they're doing. In the world of the engineer there are well-defined "rights and wrongs". And this clarity can be liberating.

The Economist

The world of the archetypal "Economist" is a very Utilitarian perspective, where a price is put on everything. When Oscar Wilde had Lord Darlington quip that a cynic was "a man who knows the price of everything and the value of nothing" he could just as easily have been describing an economist.

In the world of the economist people become a commodity. We now commonly talk about "human capital". And the corporate department which aims to maximise the return on this capital is labelled "Human Resources". This impersonal, mechanistic view sees people as being motivated by self-interest alone, and so financial incentives have become the answer to every desired change.

Everything comes with a price tag attached. Whilst the engineer aims for perfection and is concerned, say, with safety-at-all-costs, the mindset of the economist is more pragmatic. It can therefore seem a cold, impersonal, calculating outlook, one ruled by statistics and data. All too often, people are ignored or at best treated dispassionately; all too often it's a world where "The Computer says No".

The economist mindset also shapes our lives within our places of work. The view of the economist is that organisations are either growing or dying. Standing still is never an option. And so continuous Growth is seen as progress. The company must forever get bigger. And since life is clearly about competition the best way to ensure growth is to offer big rewards to the best performers. Quantity trumps quality every time.

The Artist

The world of the archetypal "Artist" is the world of creation. It's one where the focus is on matters of the heart and on feelings. Those involved do it because they want to, because they have to, not because there will necessarily be any pay-back at the end. Yes, if the result is, at some point, seen to be useful then that is a "nice to have". But utility is rarely the motivation.

Art is about turning the ordinary into the extraordinary. It's about taking seemingly trivial elements – shapes, sounds, rhythms, textures, colours, words – and somehow fashioning these basic units into a fresh, miraculous whole, whether it be a painting, building, sculpture, symphony, novel, or poem. From this perspective, Carl Jung's work could be seen as a study of how the basic units of personality create the work of art that is every human being.

Joining the dots in an innovative way, seeing new connections, discovering original patterns: these are all aspects of Creativity, the world of "surprise", that the artist thrives on. The artist flourishes as a free spirit, as a soloist. But this independent streak comes at a price. The artist is always on the outside, rarely a team-player. They're often wary of those who seek power and control, those who like to lead. And since art is about "doing" and being hands-on, the artist can also be suspicious of management, those who no longer can or want to "do".

Creativity is uncomfortable with timeframes and deadlines – producing a work of art "takes as long as it takes". And then there's the dislike of measurement, and what might loosely be termed the "scientific approach". To an artist, the fact that qualities such as Beauty, Love, and Imagination cannot be measured is part of their very attraction. It's evidence of something ineffable, of some underlying value, of some connection to an "absolute truth", a truth which can only be appreciated, rarely articulated, and never measured.

+ + +

So, why these brief Archetypal pen-portraits? Because I think they can help shine a light onto some aspects of the workplaces we spend our time in.

Clearly, the archetypal Artist doesn't fit easily into the contemporary organisational world where deadlines, measurement, teamwork, and management are valued. But the price we pay for that is that their creative, imaginative, human perspective is so often excluded.

For reasons we've discussed in earlier essays, many of our institutions continue to reflect the impersonal, mechanistic worlds of the Engineer and the Economist. Organisations are all too often viewed as being made up of a collection of interlocking parts that somehow fit together. When we draw a typical organisation chart, with a hierarchy of roles and reporting relationships, we are using a machine metaphor of the organisation. When we talk of efficiency, productivity, frameworks, targets, appraisals, driving change, re-structuring, cascading objectives, with each of these terms we are again using the metaphor of the machine. This metaphor is so deeply ingrained that many of us don't realise that we are using it. It's not that there's anything wrong with it, per se. It's just that, as a metaphor, the machine provides a limited, one-dimensional view.

The Architect

If we're looking to somehow unite these apparently disparate positions, perhaps we can look to another archetype, the "Architect", for help. Better than anyone else, the architect is the one who is able to synthesise the worlds of the Engineer, the Artist and the Economist.

Architecture is a combination of art, science and finance. Whilst it is important to design buildings with beauty and elegance, the technical expertise must also be there, together with a strong awareness of the financials, so that the project comes in successfully on time and on budget.

To begin with, the architect needs to have a comprehensive understanding of all the various engineering disciplines – structural, electrical and mechanical. And it's a prerequisite that they also understand the physical properties of the materials they're working with.

Then there is the necessary creativity. The architect is not just a designer, they are a dreamer and a doer. While acknowledging and following all the varied regulations and restrictions, the architect is able to rise above them and design spaces and buildings that arouse our emotions, that stimulate and stir us, that are awe-inspiring.

At the same time, buildings are never in isolation. There is always a context. So, the architect must have a sophisticated awareness of "place". The architect has a deep respect for surroundings, for the environment, and for ensuring that designs complement and fit in. As Frank Lloyd Wright remarked "No house should ever be on a hill or on anything. It should be of the hill. Belonging to it."

Great architecture has a profound sense of the needs of people – not only of the clients who are paying, but also of those who will eventually occupy the structure. Great buildings are always created with humans in mind. Their life-enhancing properties are their most important. As a reflection of "the human", a great building induces feelings of belonging to the place and to the structure, a sense of wholeness, a sense of inner-security.

So, my questions for you to reflect on are these:

What are the qualities of your workplace that are most life-enhancing? As a leader what can you do to develop these? How does your organisation induce feelings of belonging? How does it create a sense of wholeness? How does it provide inner security to its people?

How do you ensure that people you're responsible for feel that they are part "of the company" and not just working "in the company"? Why might this matter? What effect could this have on morale?

In your leadership role what are you doing to create a work space for your colleagues that arouses emotions, stimulates and stirs, that is awe-inspiring? What is the effect on your team? How does this make you feel?

When have you used the machine metaphor and talked of efficiency, productivity, frameworks, targets, appraisals, driving change, re-structuring, cascading objectives? How did this way of thinking help? And how did it hinder?

What qualities of The Artist are currently missing in your workplace? How might you incorporate them? What would be the advantages, for you, your colleagues, your clients?

How do you and your colleagues create something extraordinary from the ordinary? What is the effect on you and your team? What is the effect on your clients?

In your world, when does The Economist help you? On the flip side, when has a client ever experienced "The Computer says 'No'!"? What was the effect on the relationship?

When do rules restrict you and your colleagues? What effect does that have? When do rules liberate? Why is that?

What archetypes do you habitually use to view your workplace? What other ones could you use, and how might they change your perspective?

If, say, you used the archetype of A Family to view your workplace, how might that change your perspective on how people are valued and treated?

Variation 7 –
Questioning our fortune

"Birth is life's first lottery ticket."

Jeffrey Archer

A few weeks ago I was reminiscing with a school friend. Life, we agreed, has treated us pretty well.

For a start, we're both in our 60s and we're still here. We woke up this morning. That, in itself, is something to celebrate and to be hugely grateful for, because we both have friends who no longer do, who are no longer here. One day we ourselves won't be, but for the time being we are still at the party.

We also both had the great fortune of being born in and growing up in a developed country such as the UK, and the even greater fortune of being born "on the right side of the tracks" within that country. Our lives have been stable. Unlike our parents, we've never had to face the atrocities of war. We both had the benefits of good schooling, and came of age at a time when university education was still free. Subsequent opportunities were also plentiful. Jobs, for the most part, were easy to come by. Flats and houses were affordable. As I look back, it's apparent that my generation of baby-boomers have lived through a golden age that my children are unlikely to experience and my parents certainly didn't.

And what did I do to deserve these slices of good fortune? Absolutely nothing. They were given to me on a plate. Admittedly, having been granted them I then made something of them. But the fact that I ended up with them in the first place was pure serendipity.

But that's the way of life. I am not being overly modest here. I am simply recognising that luck plays a huge role in our lives, a far greater role than many of us are willing to admit.

I suppose it's natural to want to take the credit for our successes. Think of the times we hear interviews with sports people who claim that their win is the result of all their hard work. I always want to ask "What about the other 150 competitors? Didn't they work hard too?"

In my late-20s/early 30s I lived in the Far East, working in the field of broadcasting for Radio Television Hong Kong. How did that happen? How did I end up in Hong Kong? Well, I could fabricate a story of how this career choice came about through a careful orchestration of strategy and tactics. I could. But I'd be lying. I actually ended up in Hong Kong as a result of a Bedford truck breaking down in India a few months earlier. Yes, really.

I was on an overland trek taking in the highways and byways of India when, midway between Delhi and Bombay (as it then was), our vehicle died. And so, with no transport, the group of 20 was forced to break up and we all went our separate – or not-so-separate – ways. The person I paired up with for these final few days was far better travelled than I was – a Canadian who'd worked all over the world – and during our long conversations on local buses and trains she convinced me that career-opportunities could be found well beyond the confines of North Wales, my then home. I took her advice, sent off copies of my CV, and six months later I had a job in Hong Kong.

Now, I could embellish and decorate this story, but the main elements are there. And they're true. If that truck had not broken down, I would have simply reached Bombay a couple of days later and then flown back to Heathrow. I almost certainly would never have had those thought-provoking conversations, and almost certainly I would not have ended up in Hong Kong. (The story can be extended further of course. If I'd gone straight to Bombay I would never have met my wife in Hong Kong. And my children? Well, I have looked at them many times and thought "But for that broken gearbox, you would not exist!". A sobering thought.)

The job that took me to Hong Kong was with a property consultancy, Richard Ellis, which is now part of CBRE. So how did that job morph into one at Radio Television Hong Kong? Well, more good fortune. Ever since my teens I'd been a huge admirer of a Canadian pianist called Glenn Gould. Sadly, a month after I arrived in Hong Kong came the news of his premature death – he was only 50. Some weeks later I was enthusing about him to a friend after a choir rehearsal, when I discovered that she worked at Radio Television Hong Kong's classical music channel. She explained that they were planning a 4-part tribute to him. And then she added "Would you like to write it? You obviously know far more about him than we do." And that was the start of my new career. Once again, there was a huge amount of luck involved. If I'd not gone to the rehearsal, if I'd not gone to the pub, if I'd chatted to someone else. And, of course, if Glenn Gould had not died in the first place there would have been no "4-part tribute". And there would have been no career for me in broadcasting.

OK. So, these are two of my stories. But every one of us has similar tales of being presented with chances in life. The fact that you're reading this book suggests that you've probably had your fair share. Hopefully you've made the most of them. But the important thing to recognise is that you got the opportunity in the first place. Yes, you've "run with the ball". But you were given the ball to start with. Which is a lot more than some people.

My school friend, the one I mentioned earlier, the one I was reminiscing with, was recently in Cambodia. There he met Lim Kheang, a middle-aged man, who lived through the tyranny of Pol Pot and the Khmer Rouge – the so-called Killing Fields. He explained how, as a 7-year old, he was cast into the fields to work, surviving on crickets or whatever he could find to keep him alive.

Even after the war, when he was starting to make a little money, his brother stood on a land mine and lost his leg. Overnight, Kheang had to become his carer, had to look after him. It's taken Lim Kheang a life time of hard work (learning English at his own expense) to get to a point that so many of us would regard as the very minimum we'd expect out of life. His parting remark to my friend was "You were born at the right time in the right place, but for me it was just the opposite".

So, my questions for you to reflect on are these:

In what way have you been "born at the right time, in the right place"? What effect has it had on your life?

What are some of the advantages you've experienced? What are you grateful for?

Yes, you've worked hard and "run with the ball", but what are some of the balls that you've been given? What gifts has life generously bestowed upon you?

Thinking of the job you have, in how many ways did luck and good fortune play a part in you getting it? How might things have turned out? Where might you be if things had not gone so well?

What aspects of your history – your family background, your education, your upbringing – are simply down to good fortune? How have they helped you?

Which colleagues and members of your team have not had your advantages? What has each one of them achieved, despite these hardships? How can you help each colleague develop and build on their strengths?

Given the importance of luck in all our lives, how could you encourage amongst the people you lead a sense of tolerance and kindness towards those who are less gifted? What would the effect of that be?

Theme and Variations – Listening

Theme – The Experience of Listening

"One of the easiest human acts
is also the most healing.
Listening to someone. Simply listening.
Not advising or coaching,
but silently and fully listening."

Margaret J. Wheatley

I know lots of senior people in organisations who have taken Public Speaking classes. Presumably they've been attracted by the promises of being able to "Tell a story, engage the audience, leave them inspired." Or perhaps it was "Speak with more confidence, share your ideas more clearly and learn how to influence your audience to take action." Whatever it was, they quickly got their credit cards out and booked their places.

By contrast, I don't know anyone who has chosen to enrol on a course to help them become a better listener. I guess there are varied reasons for this avoidance. Firstly, as I've argued, we live in a Left Hemisphere-dominated world where being "articulate" is praised and rewarded. Secondly, Speaking has a suggestion of being more active, whereas Listening might seem more passive. Then, thirdly, there's the fact that it's easier for people to recognise that they need help Speaking because the feedback is clearer. It's very obvious when a presentation doesn't go well, or when you don't create a connection with an audience. It's far harder, on the other hand, to realise that you might be a poor listener. And fourthly, we all like to kid ourselves that we're good listeners … after all, it's difficult to be aware of our lack of awareness!

Listening to the heartbeat

Listening is a skill we're forever being encouraged to improve. Nancy Kline, in her book "Time to Think" reminds us that good decision-making comes from good thinking, and that good thinking is a result of being listened to well. And for Rowan Williams, the one-time Archbishop of Canterbury, "Leadership is trying to feel the rhythm and the heartbeat. Leadership that matters or is effective has to be listening."

But, despite these pleas, good listening continues to be as scarce as ever, most clearly in the political realm, but elsewhere too. And the result of that, sadly, is that in contemporary society cooperation and collaboration are the exception rather than the rule. Joining forces and working in partnership with people who have opposing views relies on a strong commitment to listening. It's a commitment that being competitive just doesn't demand of you. In many ways, seeing life as a contest, as a race, as a battle to be won, is the easier option. Win/Win is much more difficult to achieve than Win/Lose. It comes as no surprise, therefore, that we live in a world that prefers to ignore true partnership and instead glorifies and rewards competition.

What gets in the way of us listening?

We've all heard the saying "The reason we have two ears and one mouth is so we can listen twice as much as we speak". So far, the implication has been that we need to improve our skills in listening to others – our colleagues, our clients, our friends, our families. Well, we certainly do. But we also need to expand the definition so as to include listening to ourselves. That must always be our starting point.

Listening is important. We all know that. After all, if I want to connect with you better – whether you are my colleague, a member of my team, my boss, my client – then I clearly need to understand you better. And to do that I must make time to listen to you.

But before I can even attempt to understand you, I have to spend time understanding me. And that means listening to me – to my own thoughts, my needs, my desires, my anxieties, my fears.

It's so easy to say. And yet we all find listening difficult. But why? Why are we unable to find time for others? And why are we so reluctant to make time for ourselves?

Well, to begin with, there's Busyness – our frantic 21st century way of life that leaves little space for … well, space, actually. Sitting down and really listening to people takes time, and in our chock-a-block lives time is something we feel we're short of. (The fact that we fill our lives with stuff that doesn't really matter is something I've talked about elsewhere, as is my contention that there is always time to do what matters).

Listening also generates Fear – a fear of being out-of-control when we listen, of slowing down enough that we're able to listen; a fear of silence and pauses, of being "present"; a fear of hearing bad news, hearing unpalatable feedback; a fear of seeming to be too passive, of being too "touchy-feely"; a fear of change and letting go of our current life-style; a fear of getting too close, of intimacy; a fear of facing the unknown; a fear of "wasting time", a fear of being vulnerable. Listening creates plenty of anxiety and fear!

Another reason for not listening, perhaps, is our Ego – our own self-importance, our desire to make our mark; our belief that we know best, that our ideas are the only ones that matter; our view that we're indispensable; our desire to be needed, to be at the centre, to contribute, to problem-solve, to take action.

And now there's the additional curse of Technology – connection 24/7; communication that is more immediate and faster by the month; instant responses that preclude listening and reflection; a belief that every second must be accounted for and therefore utilised.

The Importance of Silence

The idea of "The Sabbath" is common to many religions. It's sometimes thought to be – mistakenly – a day off, a day of idleness, a day at the end of the week when we recover from the busyness of life. But, actually, the sabbath is far better viewed as a day at the start of the week, a day of preparation, a day of intended disengagement, a day of rest which we move from rather than a day of rest which we move towards. It's a day when we create our foundations. And for that we need stillness, we need calm, we need silence – not necessarily in the strict "monastic" sense, but rather in the sense of a space in which to be quiet. In the same way that a piece of music starts, not with the notes themselves but actually with the silence which precedes the notes, likewise, we need to be aware of the silence from which any conversation, any dialogue grows. That silence is a time for preparation and reflection.

Focusing on silence helps us rid ourselves of surrounding noise and the ever-present chatter of life. It's not for the faint-hearted, though. Solitude and silence can be a struggle. Solitude can expose our weaknesses, and from there it can become easy for us to lapse into loneliness. But, the positive aspects of solitude are that it strips away all the non-essentials of life, and allows us to become aware, to listen to our thoughts, to discover ourselves.

So, my questions for you to reflect on are these:

When did you last rid yourself of "noise and chatter" for any significant period of time? What was it like? What were the challenges? What did you become aware of?

Think of a concert or other live theatrical performance you've been to. When did it actually start? Was it with the first sounds? Or did it start sometime before? What part did silence play in the whole experience? How did silence add to the feelings of expectation?

Think of a significant conversation you've had. When did it actually start? With the first, hesitant words? Or sometime before? What part did silence play in that conversation?

If the Sabbath is a time to prepare rather than recover, how can you ensure you include more of it in your schedule? What effect could that have?

When have you used Busyness as an excuse for not listening? And Fear? And Ego? And Technology? What has been the cost? What could you have done differently? What might the outcome have been in each case?

When have you used your one mouth rather than your two ears? What happened? What was the effect on the other party? What was the effect on you? What could you have done differently?

When have you had a Win/Lose situation, when Win/Win would have been preferable? What happened? What was the effect on both sides? What could you have done differently? How would that have been better?

What do you do to "feel the rhythm and heartbeat" of your team? What does it do for your team? What does it do for you?

Variation 1 –
Listening like a Musician

"In English you have this wonderful difference
between listening and hearing,
and that you can hear without listening,
and you can listen and not hear."

Daniel Barenboim

For more than twenty years now, the American conductor, Roger Nierenberg, has run a programme called The Music Paradigm. It's a workshop for corporate executives designed to explore some of the many lessons of leadership that can be learned from the relationship between a Conductor and an Orchestra.

Attendees sit in on an orchestral rehearsal. But it's a rehearsal like no other. Because on this occasion they are not just audience members observing from afar. They actually take their seats amongst the performers, their chairs positioned within the orchestra. From there they are able observe at close quarters the interactions between the players and the conductor.

To read about "listening" (which, I am well aware, is what you're doing now!) is one way to approach the subject. It is probably better than nothing. It is a start. But like all cognitive learning it can easily miss the mark. On the other hand, experiencing listening, being immersed in it, having it all around you, being in the heart of it, is an event which is rarely forgotten.

A fresh seat

Throughout The Music Paradigm workshop Roger Nierenberg urges attendees to swap seats, to sit in various sections of the orchestra, and listen to the difference it makes to the sound. Those who start off amongst the violins may, for example, take a seat next to the horns. The differences are immediately apparent. Whereas the strings a few moments ago were bright and present, from this position on stage they're now distant and dull. There are also clear differences in what the two sections are asked to do, the music that they are asked to play. Whereas the strings are playing continuously, forever chattering away, the horns for much of the time seem barely occupied. There are long periods when they're not doing much at all. But, when they are, well, the volume is shattering. In those moments, brief as they may be, nothing else is audible at all. You can certainly see lots of activity in every other section, but when the four horns are playing flat out, from this vantage point you can hear nothing else.

But as soon as you move to the other side of the stage it's all change once more. Individually, cellos can't compete with horns volume-wise. But there are far more of them, probably ten in the section, so when they're all playing fortissimo it's the same story. You hear just cellos. Everything else is drowned out.

But then, finally, you get a chance to take a seat behind the podium, just at the back of the conductor. From that "front-row-of-the-audience" seat, miraculously, you can hear everything. All the sections that you've just been sitting amongst, they're all there. But, from this position, the sound is balanced, everything is in the right proportions. The different strands have had a chance to come together and mix. And suddenly the sound is brilliant and alive. As Roger Nierenberg describes, it's as if a two-dimensional photo has suddenly snapped into a three-dimensional hologram, right before your eyes.

The Podium and the Chair

But this "front-row-seat" is at ground level, the same level as the players, so visibility is still restricted. And connection is restricted. But from the podium, which is where the conductor stands, there is a whole other level of clarity. The podium may be only 18 inches or so deep, and yet that extra height plus the fact that the conductor is standing rather than sitting has an enormous effect. To begin with, from that elevated position the conductor can see people's faces and their expressions, and can make direct eye-contact with each player. The strings – the violins, violas and cellos – fan out in straight lines so that the podium becomes the focal point both visually and acoustically. The other sections – brass, woodwind, percussion and the double basses – are in blocks behind, but now freely visible from this exclusive vantage point.

But here's the problem. The transparency of sound that the conductor hears is just not available to those in the sections. So, what may be blindingly obvious to the conductor on the podium may be inaudible to the player in the chair. It's a source of continual misunderstanding. People having different perspectives. It's also tempting to assume that the Podium viewpoint, the big-picture, is "best", that it should always be the players who stretch across to embrace the conductor's reality. But the players' reality is just as valid. It's different, but still valid. Hence the conductor's need to know every part of the score. Without that knowledge it's difficult to reach across and support.

Avoiding silos

When you are sitting in the heart of a section, say the Cellos, as a listener you're immediately struck by the remarkable unanimity, the "togetherness" of the players. But this all comes at a price. The varying soundscapes which The Music Paradigm attendees experience as they move from section to section are what the players hear day-in-day-out. Instrumentalists only ever hear things from their own specific place in the orchestra. And this has consequences.

Cellists spend a lifetime studying the cello part of orchestral scores, and then playing and listening to the orchestral repertoire surrounded by other cellists. Violinists do the same. Ditto French Horn players, Bassoonists, Trumpet players, and everyone else. Over the years they all become accustomed to their own unique perspective of the orchestral world, perhaps forgetting that their view is just one of many possibilities. Unlike the workshop attendees, they rarely if ever sit elsewhere. As a result, they don't know what they don't know. They assume that everyone else hears what they hear, that everyone else experiences the same reality. But, of course, other players don't. Each section has an unbalanced view. They know their part extremely well. But they can never know the whole. (If you're seeing parallels here between sections of the orchestra and departments in your own organisation – silos such as Sales / Production / Marketing / Legal, where people have a similar monocular perspective, where they can't see or hear other views, and where they have little understanding of the "big picture" – well, these parallels are intentional.)

The one person on stage who is not right in the heart of a section, who is not in one of these instrumental silos and so is able to hear all the parts, is the conductor. First, though, they have to know all the parts. They have to learn the work from every possible angle, to know it from the point of view of each of the instruments in the orchestra. But knowing is not enough. In order to get the most from the players, to honour each of them, the conductor must listen to all of these very different points of view with intense interest and curiosity. People are reluctant to give of their best unless they know they're being listened to, being appreciated, being valued. And, as if these details weren't enough, the conductor must simultaneously have a comprehensive understanding of how the work sounds as a whole and how each of the pieces of the aural jigsaw fit together.

Foreground, Middle ground, Background

Most Music Paradigm delegates have never attended an orchestral rehearsal before. And there are surprises aplenty. The first is how the rehearsal is run, and how little talking there is. At the start, there is no agenda, no lengthy speech outlining the aim of the rehearsal, nothing about the Ground Rules we need to agree, even less explaining what the piece is about. There is just a simple "Good afternoon, Ladies and Gentlemen. Let's start with the opening Allegro." And then they're off. And most impressively, they're off together. From the very first note. And that's how it continues, with the conductor saying very little.

The next surprise is that when the conductor does talk, it's often to encourage players not to watch the baton, but instead to listen to another part – "Violins, the oboe is the focus here. Listen to how they just articulated those quavers." The beauties of this approach are many. Firstly, it encourages players to listen, without the distraction of watching. It can also be inspiring to the players to discover minute details in other parts of the score which they may never have noticed before. But most importantly, when players are encouraged to listen and when they are empowered to imitate others, their own energy becomes focused and directed. As they discover their own collective way to achieve what is needed, they rely more on their own ears and less on the conductor for feedback. But here's the rub. For the players to become less dependent, the conductor must be the one to make the first move. They have to be the one to let go, they must first relinquish some control.

One of the challenges for players in an orchestra is that they only have their own parts. Unlike singers in choirs, orchestral players don't have the whole score, so it's difficult to know what other people are doing and what to listen to at any particular time. That's where the conductor comes in. They do have the full score, and so it's their job to identify from moment to moment the focal point for the orchestra to home in on. In a simple song where there is just a tune and an accompaniment, it is straightforward to decide what is most important. But orchestral scores are multi-layered, often with twenty or more different parts playing at a time. Notwithstanding the composer's instructions, it is the conductor's role to decide how every bar should be balanced, which instruments should be most prominent and in the foreground, which should be in the middle ground, and which make up the background.

The marvel of listening

For many attendees the workshop is almost overwhelming. To begin with, there's exhilaration – the variety and immediacy of the sound, the swirling changes of focus, being that close to "the action". There is also curiosity – the variety of instruments: strings ... woodwind ... brass ... percussion, their different ranges and techniques. There is the musical language – the comments of the conductor and the reactions of the players – plus the apparent ease with which they all do what they do. For some attendees, there might even be bewilderment – "What is going on?". After all, for most people this is an alien world, undeniably pleasing, but alien all the same. But usually, as the workshop continues, any previous feelings of confusion ebb away, and are invariably replaced by a sense of wonder: "How do they perform so well? Individually they all play wonderfully – you can hear them and see them – but the real mystery is how they act as a single unit. How can they be so unified? How do they play so perfectly together, how do they play as one?"

For any organisation, one of the aims is for everyone to be pulling in the same direction, to be completely aligned. It is so basic, and it sounds so straightforward. But, of course, it isn't. Because it will only ever happen when employees feel able to speak openly and are able to express their views honestly. And they will only do that when they believe that they will be heard. And heard, not in some superficially patronising way, but heard unconditionally, in a truly respectful, honouring manner. By far the best way to promote listening in an organisation is to set ruthlessly high standards for your own listening. When attendees at Roger Nierenberg's workshops marvel at the standard of playing, in actual fact they are marvelling at the standard of listening. That is what musicians do. In the same way that visual artists – painters – know how to see, musicians know how to listen.

So, my questions for you to reflect on are these:

When have you been listened to with real interest and curiosity and respect? What was happening? Who was listening? How did it make you feel? What did you learn?

When did you last listen to each of your team with real interest and curiosity? What was going on? What did you learn about them? What did you learn about yourself?

How do you personally avoid "Silo thinking"? What do you do to learn about what other teams and departments do? How do you ensure that your view of the organisation extends beyond your own team or department?

How do you ensure your team avoids "Silo thinking"? What do you do to help them learn about what others do? How do you ensure that their view of the organisation extends beyond your own team or department?

From moment to moment conductors balance the sound of the orchestra. As a leader how do you balance your team? How do you prioritise Foreground, Middle Ground and Background? What challenges does this present? How do you cope with these?

From your "podium view" and your knowledge of the "full score" how can you help team members know who to collaborate with, who to listen to? When have you helped colleagues make these connections? What was the effect?

As a leader, from your elevated "podium view" what are you able to see that your colleagues can't? What is blindingly obvious to you but invisible to them? What could you do to share more of your view?

Variation 2 –
Listening like a Conductor

"Most people do not listen with the intent to understand; they listen with the intent to reply."

Stephen Covey

Stamping Your Own Personality is not leading

When Roger Nierenberg runs his Music Paradigm workshops, more often than not he is standing in front of an orchestra that he doesn't know. The reason for this is simple logistics. As I write this, in recent weeks he has visited San Francisco, Seattle, Miami and London. Obviously, no Organisational Learning & Development budget would allow him to cart a Symphony orchestra around the world, so he simply hires one locally for the day.

We've seen how attendees are often surprised at how little talking there is, especially at the start of the session. The reason for this now becomes a little clearer. The first thing conductors do when they play with an orchestra is LISTEN. They are not there to "explain the piece", or to tell the orchestra about their vision of the work, their "interpretation", or to give the orchestra a "Music Appreciation" lecture. And neither are they there to immediately stamp their personality on the group. The conductor's first job is to let the orchestra play.

When conductors arrive for a first rehearsal, naturally they are expected to know the piece and have a clear vision of what they want. But at the same time, they recognise that the orchestra or choir is not some "tabula rasa" upon which they simply impose their views. As I've already explained, one of the challenges for a conductor standing in front of a professional orchestra is that the players in many ways know the piece better than the conductor does. They will have played most works in the standard repertoire – Mozart, Beethoven, Brahms, Tchaikovsky – countless times over the years, to the point where there is probably a "house interpretation" of the work – an amalgam, if you like, of all the past interpretations they've experienced. Any conductor would be a fool to ignore such knowledge and ideas that already exist. And so the first part of any rehearsal is always going to be spent getting to know what's going on in the orchestra. And the conductor does that by letting the group play and allowing the ideas to come to the fore.

And as they do, the conductor watches and listens to what's happening: and will be asking him or herself "What's the 'house interpretation' like? Which ideas match my own and which are different? Which are better and which are worse? Which ideas need to be amplified and which dampened? What's the natural sound of the group? What do the players do easily and what do they find difficult? Which sections of the orchestra are stronger and which are weaker? How well are they playing together and listening to each other?" And gradually things become clearer: what needs to be corrected immediately, and what can be ignored for the time being. Of course, the conductor has the authority to make these decisions, but it's on the tacit understanding that he works with the group, not against it.

The conductor's key skill, then, is their ability to listen. That's their principal mode of inspiration and persuasion. Of course, the conductor must also have a good "stick technique" – ie: be able to communicate their ideas using the baton. And they must have thorough musical knowledge. But for the players to give of their best they need to feel that they've been heard and listened to by the conductor, that their contributions are appreciated and valued. As the saying goes, People don't care what you know until they know that you care.

Likewise, in organisational life, the purpose of leadership is first to listen and discover through dialogue what's going on within the group of people you're responsible for. A large part of the role of Leadership is asking the right questions, thereby unearthing the ideas that are already bubbling around in the organisation – on the production line, in the sales force, in the legal team, in marketing – to make things more efficient / safer / friendlier / better for the customer.

Leadership is also about listening to what's going on outside of the organisation. What "new trends" have people spotted? What's the next "big thing"? There's a sobering tale from around the year 2000 which tells how Nokia almost missed the boat with regard to Text Messaging. Middle-aged senior leaders, who presumably thought that phones were only for talking on, viewed Texts as of peripheral interest and couldn't see the benefits. Fortunately, these same managers were open to listening to younger colleagues who persuaded them that SMS was the future. And it was! (Sadly, for Nokia, a few years later when the next big innovation hit the mobile world in the form of Smartphones, this time they DID miss the boat. But that's another story!)

Obviously not all ideas can be implemented immediately. Having listened to everyone's views and ideas choices have to be made, and it's the role of the Leader to use their authority, their "positional power", to make these choices – to choose which already-existing initiatives need to be amplified (and which should be dampened, at least for the time being) and then to co-ordinate it all happening.

Pushing is not Leading

At one time or another, we've probably all been on the receiving end of the words "Don't just stand there. Do something!". In a world where speed and results and achieving are prized so greatly, all at the expense of reflection and thought and context, this phrase now resonates more than ever. As opposed to allowing things to emerge, letting things occur in their own time, many of us feel the need to take action, to make our presence felt, to provide Added Value. After all, that's what we're there for, isn't it?. We're leaders. We're doers. We make things happen.

When I learned to fly, almost the first thing I was shown by the instructor was just how little effort it takes. As a pilot you are not there to put energy into making the plane take off. The plane does it all for you. Planes are built to fly. Getting an aircraft off the ground is effortless. Having lined up at the end of the runway, all you do is put the engine to full power and release the brakes. As the aircraft accelerates away, you steer it in a straight line, and when the plane reaches 65 knots you use the slightest pressure imaginable to pull back on the control column, and up you go. Actually, even if you did nothing, the plane will take off. The plane wants to fly, and, apart from switching the engine off, there's little you could do at that speed to keep it on the ground.

And when it's airborne the plane is even more in its element. Once it's trimmed and set up correctly it will fly "straight and level" very happily without any input from the pilot. In fact, everyone's first lesson includes a "Look, No Hands" demonstration by the instructor to show how the plane flies itself. No, the pilot is not there to create or indeed use any power. They're there to direct it. And they should direct it using the minimum of effort. Less is always More.

The same goes for a professional orchestra. They're designed to play, to perform. That's what they do. They can "take off" perfectly well without the conductor. And once they're "airborne" any external inputs should always be the minimum possible. An experienced conductor simply lets the players fly.

Micromanaging is not Leading

I've already stated the obvious, that the conductor must know what the orchestra is playing – ie: know the score – completely, and better than anyone else. But what is actually involved in knowing the score?

Well, the way I would describe it is that conductors must know the score and be able to listen both "horizontally" and "vertically". By horizontally I'm referring to the marks on the page – all the various hieroglyphics that composers use to attempt to put onto paper the musical sounds that they hear in their heads. To begin with there are the notes themselves, all different lengths (eg: minims, crotchets, quavers) all at various pitches (from high to low). But then performers need to know the volume to play, so the score often contains a host of dynamic marks (forte, piano and the like) suggesting how loud or quiet a particular note should be, plus other marks indicating whether a phrase gradually gets louder or softer over time. Then there are numerous articulation marks (staccato, tenuto, marcato) which show whether the notes should be played with a certain attack or, perhaps, more smoothly. And then the players need to know how fast the piece goes, so there are tempo indications (allegro, andante, presto, accelerando, ritardando) all of which signify the overall speed of the piece as well as showing where it slows down or speeds up.

Before standing in front of the orchestra the conductor must have considered every single one of these symbols and features of the score (plus countless others) and put them all together, like some vast 10,000 piece jigsaw, to create a unified whole. Only when they know it in that sort of detail can they then listen to this "horizontal" aspect of the music. But that's only part of their job. There's more. In addition, the conductor needs to know how the score fits together "vertically", by which I mean they must know how all these numerous horizontal strands interweave and interact at any given moment. If you remember, we've already discussed how, rather than instructing the orchestra in some sort of didactic manner, it's better to encourage the orchestra to listen to each other – "Violins, the oboe is the focus here. Listen to how they just articulated those quavers". Well, to help the players collaborate and listen in this way the conductor has to decide at every moment what would be the most helpful part for them to focus on, what bit of this ever-changing soundscape needs to come to the fore. The conductor has to continually listen vertically, balancing the orchestra – prioritising what is most important at any particular time, making decisions regarding background, middle ground and foreground.

So, the conductor must know everything possible about the score. And it's important that the players can see this knowledge. Because it will make them feel safe and they will then be able to give of their best. But here's the crucial thing. The conducting must never demonstrate that knowledge. Yes, the players need to recognise that the conductor knows every detail. But they don't want the conductor to focus on every detail. Unless the work is new and complicated and particularly challenging, there is no place for micromanagement in an orchestra. If the conductor tries to direct every note, the message to the players is that they're not trusted to do their jobs. They will feel stifled and suppressed and belittled. They will think that their wings have been clipped.

Cheerleading is not Leading

All professional instrumentalists are pretty remarkable when it comes to technique. Not only have they been blessed with the gift of natural talent but as we have previously seen, they have then, from a very young age, worked on it and practised for way more than the "10,000 hours" that Malcolm Gladwell suggests it takes to reach mastery. As well as the listening abilities we've talked of, they've all developed extraordinary motor skills in their hands, and at the highest levels can show a seemingly infinite range of power and subtlety and speed.

But there's one group of instrumentalists that I have a special admiration for, and that is Cathedral Organists. Yes, every instrument has its own peculiar challenges. But you usually need no more than two hands to overcome them. Organists, by contrast, have to contend with an additional musical line played on the pedals, an extra keyboard played by the feet. Given that many people find patting their head and rubbing their tummy at the same time quite a test, the feat of playing a Bach Fugue on the organ is unimaginable.

Conductors, however, face a comparable challenge, albeit one that is more cerebral. They have to listen and act in multiple ways concurrently. For the conductor to be able to direct the orchestra their gestures, including the movement of the baton, must occur before the sound – if the gestures occur at the same time as the sound, then the conductor is not actually leading, they're following. But before the gestures can be made the conductor needs to hear the idealised sound in their head. So, in effect, they are operating in three time zones simultaneously. At any single moment they are hearing the orchestra and responding to "what is" – ie: what is actually being played – noticing what needs to be corrected and encouraging what's going well. Then, at the same time, their gestures are anticipating the sounds, indicating to the orchestra what is coming up in the bars ahead, what is about to happen, where they're going next. And, finally, in their mind the conductor is even further ahead, imagining and committing to their ideal performance, which is what will inspire the players to give of their best. It's an intellectual achievement akin to simultaneous translation. It's hard work. And it's uncomfortable. It would be far more comfortable to be with the orchestra, to be in time with them. But then the conductor wouldn't be leading. As Roger Nierenberg explains "If the conductor is merely affirming what the players are already doing, it amounts to little more than cheerleading."

So, my questions for you to reflect on are these:

As a leader, what future have you committed to? How do you continually share that vision with your people? How does that 100% commitment energise them? How do they react to your vision of "what's possible"?

When have you focused too much on past results? When have you affirmed the team's behaviours and been a Cheerleader rather than a Leader? What could you have done differently? What effect might this have had?

When have you ever micro-managed a situation? Describe a time when it helped your people. Why did they need that level of help? How did they benefit? How did they feel afterwards?

Describe a time when micro-management was not the best approach. Why did you choose to Manage rather than Lead? What was the effect on people? Did they feel trusted? Did they feel their wings had been clipped? How could you have got out of the detail and shown them the big-picture?

What, for you, is the difference between Pushing and Leading? In your organisational environment, in what ways could you apply the principle of "Less is More"? Why don't you? What do you need to let go of?

Describe a time when, as a leader, you "got in the way". What was the situation? What could you have done differently that would have allowed your team to fly? Rather than creating and using your own energy, how could you direct the team's energy?

When have you attempted to "stamp your mark" on your team? Was it a successful strategy? Why did you feel the need to do that? Is that what "Strong Leadership" looks like to you?

If you'd focused more on the people you lead rather than on your own actions, if you listened first to all the members of the team, in what ways might your decisions have been different? How might that have changed the outcome?

Variation 3 –
The Price of Not Listening

"Don't assume, because you are intelligent,
able, and well-motivated, that you are open to
communication, that you know how to listen."

Robert K. Greenleaf

In the world of Health and Safety, High Hazard Industries are those where the control of major hazards is absolutely critical, where the price of a malfunction is extremely high. Not only can they be risky places for employees, but the results of any failure would extend well beyond the perimeters of the workplace and can be catastrophic for the population at large. High Hazard industries, be they Nuclear Power, Oil & Gas, Mining, Mass transport, Construction, Space travel, are ones where an attitude of "95% is good enough" is NOT good enough. They are ones where we hope the organisation really does believe that "Safety is our #1 priority."

In such industries, accidents are, thankfully, extremely rare. But they do happen. And they're usually very public. We can all remember the Gulf of Mexico Oil spill in 2010, and the nuclear melt-downs at Chernobyl and Fukushima, and the two Space Shuttle disasters in 1986 and 2003. As I write this in the spring of 2019, Boeing has very publicly grounded all its 737 Max planes following two recent crashes. It's difficult to hide accidents in High Hazard industries.

I used the word "accident" just then. But that is actually misleading. Because in the world of Disaster Investigations, there is a preference to use the word "Incident". "Accident" implies something unknown, unforeseen, unexpected. But these large-scale disasters are rarely like that. Almost every time they are the result of a coming-together of numerous factors, all of which are known, all of which have occurred before, all of which have been documented before, all of which have been talked about endlessly in meetings. And none of which have been learned from. And why? Because people heard but they didn't listen.

Space Shuttles

The two Space Shuttle disasters are a case in point. We've all seen the "Challenger" footage from 1986 – the seven smiling crew members, including the teacher Sharon McAuliffe, walking out to their transit bus, then the lift-off and initial ascent from Cape Canaveral, then, 73 seconds into the flight, the explosion and breakup of the launch vehicle.

17 years later in 2003, NASA suffered its second Shuttle disaster when Columbia broke up on re-entry. The footage of this is perhaps less dramatic – there are no visuals of the explosion itself given that the vehicle was still 38 miles up. What we see is Mission Control. And the simple, repeated request by the Ground Communicator trying to make contact following the usual radio blackout: "Columbia, Houston, UHF Comm check ... Columbia, Houston, UHF Comm check".

In many ways the two disasters were completely different – one occurred on lift-off, the other on re-entry. One was to do with "O-Rings", the other with "Insulation tile damage". But at the same time, in the words of Prof Julianne Mahler, there were "chilling similarities". In both situations, investigators found that decision makers were isolated, and they failed to listen to either in-house or contract engineers who expressed concerns about the problem elements. Before both accidents, flight managers were under extreme pressure from Congress and the public to maintain launch schedules, and they had not followed established procedures for clearing unresolved problems. The Columbia Accident Investigation Board actually concluded that NASA was not a learning organisation. Which is another way of saying that it was not a listening organisation.

Texas City

Wednesday 23 March 2005 began as just another day at BP's oil refinery in Texas City. But by lunchtime 15 people would be dead and 180 injured when a cloud of highly flammable gas which had engulfed much of the site was ignited, causing an explosion and fireball which destroyed a large part of the refinery. Once again, this "accident" was no accident at all. Both the BP and the U.S. Chemical Safety and Hazard Investigation Board reports identified numerous technical and organisational failings at the refinery and within corporate BP – failings to do with equipment, risk management, staff management, working culture, maintenance and inspection, and general health and safety assessments.

One of the by-products of refining petroleum is gas, but this waste is routinely burned off for environmental and safety reasons. We've probably all driven past oil refineries and seen, especially at night, a huge flare which is getting rid of excess gas. Well, back in the 1950s, when Texas City was built, flares were the exception rather than the rule. Open vents, where the gas just dispersed straight out into the atmosphere, were deemed satisfactory. By the 1990s, standards had changed. Or at least, they had changed for new refineries. But Texas City remained as it was. It had no flares, just vents. That's how a large gas cloud was able to occur in the first place. With a flare any excess gas would have burned off. But in Texas City it collected on the ground in a great cloud. And then the cloud was ignited. And then ... well, it ripped the place apart.

But here's the thing. This was by no means the first time a cloud of gas had ever formed. It was actually a fairly regular occurrence. In the previous decade there had been at least six similar documented instances of this happening. And all at this very same refinery in

Texas City! The only difference on the previous six occasions was that there was no ignition source, so they got away with it. Apart from that, though, the conditions were the same. So, people knew that this was an ever-present danger. They documented it. They logged it. They had meetings about it. But nobody learned from past mistakes. Once again, people heard but they didn't listen. And 15 people died.

I suppose this inability to listen and learn from the past should come as no surprise. After all, it was ever thus. As Hegel asserted in 1832, "What experience and history teach is this — that people and governments never have learned anything from history, or acted on principles deduced from it."

So, my questions for you to reflect on are these:

When have you personally not listened and learned? What could you have
learned from the situation? What pain would you have avoided?

What was the cost to yourself? And to others ... family, friends, colleagues?

When has your team not listened and learned? What could the team have
learned from the situation? What pain would the team have avoided?

What was the cost to the team? And to others?

When has your organisation not listened and learned? What should it have learned from the situation? What would have been avoided?

What was the cost to the organisation? How was its reputation affected? What was the cost to others? How were clients/customers affected? What could you have done differently?

Theme and Variations – Changing

Theme – The Experience of Change

"Plus ça change, plus c'est la meme chose."

French proverb

Every year Corporations and Institutions spend fortunes on all manner of "change programmes" and "change initiatives" with the aim of altering the behaviours of their people and improving the financial standing of the organisation. Whilst there are undoubted successes, it's not everyone's experience. The above French proverb – "The more things change, the more they stay the same" – sums up how many people view their place of work. It speaks to the immutability of organisational life, and it communicates, with an air of resignation, that whilst superficial things may change, nothing of substance ever does. Things change but things remain static.

This belief, that "organisational stasis" is the norm, underpins many leadership theories, and gives rise to the idea that leadership is fundamentally about "change", about moving people from where they are to where those with power think they should be, whether the people want to be moved or not! Unsurprisingly therefore, change in organisations is perceived to be unwelcome and difficult. And so there have to be "programmes" and "initiatives", all designed to "help" (or could that be "force"?) people to adapt to whatever new environment the organisation finds itself in. And just in case encouragement is needed, ideally there should be a charismatic leader who motivates and persuades so that change actually happens.

This idea that leaders somehow "make change happen" can be very seductive. Early in January 2019 the English football team, Manchester United, enjoyed a great run of form. Having had a somewhat lacklustre start to the season – actually not that poor, given that they were still 6th out of 92 teams in the Football League – they sacked their manager Jose Mourinho and appointed the Norwegian coach, Ole Gunnar Solskjær, as caretaker manager. Immediately their form changed and they had a run of eight straight wins. It goes without saying that Solskjær was talked about as if he was the new Messiah, as if he had magical powers, as if this new-found success was all down to him.

This straightforward and rather black-and-white view of "cause and effect" is enticing. And it can be seen running through various theories of change. Back in 1951 the American psychologist, Kurt Lewin, created one of the most enduring models of change. Often described as the "Unfreeze, Change, Refreeze" model, there were two main assumptions: firstly, the agency of a powerful leader and, secondly, the static nature of organisations. The basic concept is a simple one. If you have a big block of ice and want to transform it into a new shape then you first need to unfreeze the block, then pour the water into a mould and finally refreeze it. Likewise in an organisation, if you want to move from Point A to Point B, then you first need to "unfreeze" certain beliefs and behaviours. Then you can implement a "change" phase. And, finally, once you have reached Point B you then need to "refreeze" and normalise the new behaviours and beliefs.

In essence, the suggestion is that movement is from a Steady State → a Change State → Steady State, the assumption being that for individuals and organisations the steady state is the norm.

This steady-state idea also underpins another well-established change methodology, namely John Kotter's 8-step model of change. It forms the basis of his book "Leading Change", which was published in 1996, and has since enjoyed wide popularity. Once again, an assumption of the model is that there will be an organisational leader whose role it is to:

- Create a Sense of Urgency
- Build a Guiding Coalition
- Form a Strategic Vision and Initiatives

- Enlist a Volunteer Army
- Enable Action by Removing Barriers
- Generate Short-Term Wins
- Sustain Acceleration
- Institute Change

There are a number of things to say about this model and its assumptions. To start with, its top-down view of leadership, one where a single leader "Builds a coalition" and "Forms a vision" and "Enlists an army" and "Enables action" sits rather awkwardly with the model of distributed leadership that we've been examining thus far. And then there's the "steady-state" view of organisational life that assumes that change generally doesn't happen unless it is encouraged or perhaps even imposed.

But is the world around us static? What if it is far more fluid than it appears? After all, isn't this what mystics and philosophers and physicists have been telling us for years, for centuries? For them, it is clear that Change is the norm. It's everywhere, and it's forever happening. It might not always seem that way, but that's because we're looking at the change through our eyes and judging its speed and its rate of change by our standards. Let's take the idea of Continental Drift, for example. For decades, now, we've understood that the surface of the earth has shifted over millions of years. We recognise that what we now call South America and Africa used to be joined together. We know that the Himalayan mountain range has been pushed upwards as a result of the Indian sub-continent "slamming" up against the main block of Asia. We're all happy to talk about Tectonic Plates. But when we do there's still a tendency to imagine that these movements happened at some time "in the past" and that things are now static. But they're not static. The Himalayas are in a state of constant flux. Every day they're being worn down by erosion whilst at the same time still being pushed up by tectonic movement. They're on the move all the time: it's just that our minds can't register such slow movement. The speed of change is too imperceptible for us to notice.

If movement then, not stasis, is the norm, and we think back to Kurt Lewin, where does that leave his "Unfreeze, Change, Refreeze" model? If everything is always on the move, how do you select a Point A? Where exactly is "here" and where is "now"? And then looking forward, how do you establish a Point B to aim at? And in this ever-changing world what happens in the interim, in the "change phase"? How do you know that you've reached Point B? If you believe life to be a process, something that is forever flowing and changing like a river, is it an illusion to believe you can ever stop it?

With all these unanswered – perhaps unanswerable? – questions, the next chapter will delve a bit deeper. In the meantime, my questions for you to reflect on are these:

What are some of the traditional change initiatives you've experienced in your organisational life? What were their aims?

Which were "successful"? How successful were they? How was the success measured?

Why were they successful? In whose eyes were they successful? What happened? What didn't happen?

Which initiatives were less successful? In whose eyes? In what way did they fail?

Why did they fail? What was done? What was not done?

What would you have done differently? What would have been the benefits?

Variation 1 –
The Gestalt view of Change

"Change is only another word for growth,
another synonym for learning."

Charles Handy

There is clearly a traditional view of how we like to believe that change happens. It's simple really. All we need to do is …

- See where we are
- Establish where we want to be
- Put a plan in place
- Take action

It's so straight-forward. And it's so pervasive a view that we've probably all bought into it at one time or another. Think of the month of January after the Christmas feasting. Who hasn't, once or twice, caught a glimpse of themselves in the mirror and been so shocked by the image, that they've resolved that something has to be done? In your mind's eye you imagine a "new you", a rather more svelte version of you, and conclude that some weight needs to be lost. You make a plan and choose a fresh dietary regime – Atkins, 5/2, Low-fat, Low-carb, Vegetarian, Vegan – and, to give yourself some extra impetus, you book yourself into the nearest gym as an added measure. And then, for the next three months you take massive action and, hey presto, you end up with the body of your dreams.

That's how we like to think it will work. And even though we know it doesn't – after all, none of us have ever got to Easter looking like an Olympic swimmer – we kid ourselves that this time it will be different, presumably because we'll "be more focused, have clearer goals, work harder." And, to be fair, we might well lose some weight over the months. But is it as a result of the new regime, or would we have lost the weight anyway? And even if we do lose some weight initially, does it ever go back on? Of course it does, because the excess weight was just a symptom of an underlying problem that has yet to be fixed.

As we saw in the previous essay – and as many of us know from our own organisational experiences – this model of change is also the norm in our workplaces. We know it's a flawed idea, and we know that previous initiatives have rarely, if ever, delivered on their promises. But, ever the optimists, we carry on instigating yet more Change Management Programmes. Each time we convince ourselves that "we've now ironed out past problems, been more precise on the deliverables, and we've sharpened up the processes". In other words, we pretend that "This time it will be different".

As I've mentioned previously, in 1970 the American psychiatrist and Gestalt therapist, Arnold Beisser, wrote a short article entitled "The Paradoxical Theory of Change" in which he proffered a rather different model from the one we're used to. With just a single sentence – and a very innocuous sounding one at that – he turned the traditional world of "change" on its head. Beisser's view of a client wanting to change was that ...

> "Change occurs when one becomes what he is,
> not when he tries to become what he is not."

Beisser continued: "Change does not take place through a coercive attempt by the individual or by any other person to change him, but it does take place if one takes the time and effort to be what he is – to be fully invested in his current positions. By rejecting the role of change agent, we make meaningful and orderly change possible."

The implications for those who have any responsibility for others – that includes therapists, coaches, consultants, team leaders, members of the Exec team, actually all of us! – is that "agency" is ineffective. Whilst coercion may produce some small temporary gains, you can't force lasting change to occur. Instead, your role is to create the environment and the conditions where change is allowed to happen naturally.

What happens if we do try to force change? Well, we quickly come up against the "paradox" in the title of the article, which is that the more we attempt to be who we are not, the more we remain the same. This applies as much to organisations as it does to us as individuals. If and when we can identify with our current experience and come to terms with who we are as an organisation, when we fully accept our Right Hemisphere's view of "what is" rather than our Left Hemisphere's view of "how we would like things to be", that's when there is the possibility of lasting change. We first must become our truth. Only then can we move from it.

It might sound easy enough, but self-examination – where we question our motives and actions, strip away our defences, challenge our whole sense of identity – makes us extremely vulnerable and is an uncomfortable business. Before we can construct something new, we first need to de-construct the existing. Before we can move forwards we first need to step backwards – back to who or what we are.

And then there's the fact that self-examination and the change that flows from it is time consuming – there are no real short cuts. Sadly, organisations tend to go for the "quick fix" and are rarely prepared to embark on this journey of self-exploration, a journey which is probably much longer and more turbulent than imagined. The result is that, like the Yo-Yo dieter whose success is temporary, any "quick-fix" changes within the organisation will be short-lived.

So, my questions for you to reflect on are these:

When have you tried to force change in your own life?
What exactly did you try to do?

Why were you doing it? What was the underlying problem?
What was lacking or not going right for you?

What did it feel like to try and force change? On a scale of 1–10, how
successful was your attempt? Could it have been better? Could you really
have "tried harder, had clearer goals, been more focused"?

When else have you noticed the "paradox" – that the more you tried to change the more things stayed the same? What was going on?

When have you tried to force change on someone else? Who was it?
A colleague? A friend? A family member?

Why were you doing it? What was the underlying problem?
How is it that you were so sure that you knew what was best for them?

How did they react to your suggestions? How did the intervention play out?
Did either of you think it was successful?

In each of the above examples, how might you have focused more on
"What is" instead of "How it should be"? What would that have looked like?

In each case, what might the long-term results have been?

Variation 2 – Process and Change

"Life is a process of becoming, a combination of
states we have to go through."

Anais Nin

Over the years I've had the good fortune to perform in many great
concert venues, but none is more memorable than the magnificent
open-air Amphitheatre at Ephesus, the ancient Greek city in what
is now modern Turkey. I had wanted to visit Ephesus for many years,
attracted by its famous sites – the nearby Temple of Artemis, one of
the Seven Wonders of the Ancient World; the Library of Celsus;
and the venue of our concert, the 25,000-seat Amphitheatre with
its famed acoustics. But I was drawn to Ephesus for another reason.
Ephesus was home to Heraclitus, the philosopher celebrated for his
assertion that change is the fundamental essence of the universe.
This belief, which has always seemed to me to be the way things are,
was summed up in his saying:

"No man ever steps in the same river twice."

… words which speak to the idea of "becoming" and to the
philosophical concept of "being". As such, it is no surprise that
Heraclitus is commonly considered to be one of the founding fathers
of ontology – the philosophy of what it is to "be".

Heraclitus was what we might call the first of the "process"
philosophers, those who believe that "stasis" is actually an illusion.
For process philosophers, transformation is the norm, everything is
perpetually moving, and any attempt to "freeze" a moment in time
immediately diminishes the richness of the experience. We all know
this to be true. Every one of us has taken photographs at some
important instant in our lives – a performance, a special evening

with friends, a romantic walk, a sunset – hoping to capture the magic for eternity. And later, we've all had to admit that whilst the images can jog our memories, they don't come close to conveying what we actually experienced at the time.

The same thing happens in the workplace in traditional Change programmes. We choose some arbitrary Point A to start from – in other words, we take a snapshot of "Where we are". But this image is usually far from the complete truth. Whole dimensions are missing. All the richness and colour associated with our lives in the workplace have been left out. We then do the same with Point B – "Where we want to be" – but invariably end up with another lifeless snapshot devoid of sensations and feelings.

Focusing on Point B has an added problem: it assumes that the end point, the goal, is all-important. But what about the "journey" to get there, what about the space between Points A and B? Imagine you went to a concert to hear a Beethoven symphony and all you heard were the first and last chords of the piece. Not only would you feel cheated, you'd know that it's complete madness. The fact that the 2nd Symphony starts in D major and ends in D major tells us nothing. What is interesting is what Beethoven does in between the start and the finish. It's how Beethoven connects those two moments that matters.

Taking Heraclitus' image of the flowing river, process philosophers see life as an ever-shifting, undivided, connected, seamless flow as opposed to a series of discreet moments. As we've seen in earlier chapters, our left hemisphere gives us the ability to reduce this seamless whole down to a collection of parts. Just to be clear once again, there is nothing inherently wrong in this. This ability can be extremely useful. Breaking things down into components can help us understand, and grasp, and manipulate and influence the world around us. But, we must always remember that it's not what reality "is". A movie film with its individual frames can give the illusion of reality but it clearly is not reality. We need to remember that the left hemisphere's separated, reductionist view of the world is also not real. It's an illusion. It's not how life "is".

The notion of "becoming", which I mentioned earlier, has a number of implications for change within organisations. As we've seen, two organisational theorists – Robert Chia and Haridimos Tsoukas – advocate that instead of talking about organisational change, we should actually talk about organisational "becoming". Not only does this acknowledge the presence of constant flux within organisations but it also hints at what the role of leadership might be if it's not, as we've discussed, to "make change happen".

In the next essay, we'll examine three roles of leadership within change. For the moment, however, my questions for you to reflect on are these:

> *When you look back 10, 20, 30 years over your own life, and think of stasis and change, what parts of you have changed? How are your behaviours and attitudes different from back then?*

> *What are the reasons for the changes? Is it just "maturity"? What are some of the life events – marriages, births, bereavements, illnesses – that have shaped you? What changes did they bring about in you?*

> *What parts of you – behaviours, outlooks, attitudes – are exactly the same as they were decades ago? Would old friends see you as "unchanged"?*

When have you tried to "freeze" time, and capture a magic moment on film? How successful were you? How much of the "magic" did you manage to capture?

What was not captured? What was missing?

When have you been so focused on capturing something for eternity that you forgot to experience it "in the moment"?

How are your answers to these personal questions reflected in the way you show up in the workplace, in the "work you"?

If the essence of a Beethoven symphony is what goes on between the start and end points, what is the essence of your team's work? Is it just about the difference between two arbitrary Points A and B – say, this year's figures and next year's figures – or is it something more?

Given the idea of "organisational becoming", what is your team becoming? What would you like it to become? What would each of your team like it to become?

Variation 3 –
The role of leadership in Change

"Leaders don't complain about what's not working.
Leaders celebrate what is working
and work to amplify it."

Simon Sinek

If I'm arguing, as I am, that the role of leadership is not really about providing the vision (ie: is NOT about identifying a Point B to aim at), and it's not really about directing new initiatives, and neither is it about making change happen, then it begs the question: "Well, what is leadership for?"

From a Process perspective, Leadership has three roles:

1. Identifying patterns

The first role of leadership is to identify patterns by seeing what others are not seeing, by hearing what others are not hearing. Organisational life can be overpowering – the general "noise", the speed, the lack of time, the amount of information to be assimilated. All too easily it can become overwhelming. But leadership is there to help us make collective sense of it all.

It's important, here, to remember the notion of "distributed leadership" that we've discussed. Leadership resides not just in the C-Suite but throughout the organisation, at all levels. Everyone can be and should be involved. Everyone's perspective is unique and potentially useful. Indeed, it's often the more junior and younger staff in customer-facing roles – receptionists, telephonists, call-centre operators – who are the first to know what is going on for the clients. Sometimes, the higher up in the building we sit – the closer we are to the C-Suite – the more disconnected we can become.

But whilst the view "on the ground" is hugely important, so too is the overview, the context into which everything fits, the overall picture. The challenge for most of us is that we only ever see our part of the organisation, so it's hard to know how our piece of the jigsaw contributes to the whole. It's as if we're trying to build the jigsaw but without ever seeing the picture on the box.

This is where leadership comes to the rescue. In the same way that the conductor of an orchestra is the one person on stage who can hear everything, who gets a balanced view, who can see more than anyone else, and can hear more, senior people in organisational life have a similarly privileged position, a "helicopter view" of the terrain. Plus, they're not bogged down in the "doing, doing, doing" that many of their team are. Like the orchestral conductor who actually doesn't have to "play the notes", organisational leaders hopefully have plenty of spare mental bandwidth to attend fully to "what is".

Some years ago I worked with an American business leader. He was recently retired but in his day he'd been a CEO of three large organisations over a fifteen year period. When I asked him about his role as a leader his response was immediate: "My role in those 15 years was to support my people. I was NOT there to be the hero and do everything myself. My colleagues were the ones doing the work, so my job was to encourage and help them in whatever way I could. And one of the things I was able to provide for them was the overall view. I could help them see how their contribution fitted into the whole."

Leadership is there to help people, to assist them. By asking the right questions – as opposed to providing the answers – leadership supports people in understanding how their work contributes to the whole. To be effective, leadership needs distance, so that it is possible to see what is going on. Those in senior roles – the "conductors", if you like – by dint of their position, have this helicopter view that I've just mentioned. They see the whole scene. From this altitude they see the bigger picture. At the same time, they cannot see all the details, and actually as Iain McGilchrist might argue, neither should they. They should not get involved in all the details, in all the minutiae. Their role is to have a broader perspective. That way they see what most others don't. They get a chance to hear what most others can't. And that allows them to spot patterns, and sort the "wheat from the chaff", differentiate the emerging trends from the surrounding noise.

2. Amplifying, dampening and declaring

In the model of change that I am putting forward, organisations are continually "becoming". Once the patterns have been spotted and the emerging trends noticed, priorities then have to be set and choices need to be made. The organisation can't and probably shouldn't respond to everything. There may well be a hundred things the organisation could do, a hundred initiatives it could follow, a hundred directions it could go in. But it has to be selective. Some trends will need to be encouraged, while others will need to be discouraged. Some will need to be amplified, others dampened or suppressed. Deciding which are the most important trends relies on having as broad a view of the whole as possible.

Once these decisions about which trends need to be amplified and dampened have been made, it's then a matter of asking the Who, How, When, Where, What questions. Who needs help? How can they be enabled? When do they need to be supported? Where are resources required? When must they be provided by? ... and so on.

And once patterns have been noticed and priorities made, it's then important that leaders "nail their colours to the mast" and declare their views and findings in a way that fully engages their people. If it's Good News then all is well and you're in for an easy ride. On the other hand, if the truths are unpleasant, if the messages are ones that people aren't going to want to hear, then as the messenger you're facing an uncomfortable journey.

3. Being disruptive

What if we see trends within the system and nobody is willing to listen? What if the emerging ideas are so unpalatable that they're dismissed? What options are open to us then?

In recent years Disruption has become a buzz-word. But as a mode of change it has always been around. In 1908 Henry Ford's mass-produced Model T car was a disruptive innovation, because it changed the transportation market. Fast-forward a century, however, and it seems as if we're now living in a period of accelerated disruption. Indeed, "disruptive innovation" has been called the most influential business idea of the early 21st century. And examples are everywhere, from Amazon to Uber, from Airbnb to Netflix. Traditional business models are being turned on their head, encouraged by a public mistrust of "the old" and a hunger for "the new".

So, my questions for you to reflect on are these:

Amidst all the inevitable "noise" how do you help your colleagues make sense of what is going on in your organisation?

As a leader, what are some things your "helicopter view" enables you to see? What are the benefits of this?

Which of your people have most connection with customers? What could you learn from them? How can you make that happen?

What could you potentially learn from colleagues who are 10, 15, 20 years your junior? How can you ensure that such learning takes place?

How do you avoid a "silo mentality" within sub-teams? How can you act as the "conductor" and help them work together more effectively?

When have you "been the hero" and done everything yourself, and when have you "simply" supported and helped? How did these situations compare?

What are some of the emerging trends in your organisation?
What is your organisation becoming?

Which trends should be amplified and which should be dampened?
What would the effects be?

How could your team and organisation be affected by disruption? What is
the potential "Uber" in your field? How can you avoid being disrupted?

Coda

"We must always remember
to learn from yesterday, live for today, and hope
for tomorrow because time will only show
what has mattered throughout our journey."

Melanie Klein

A reason to be deeply hopeful

In several earlier essays I've mentioned my Desert-Island book, Iain McGilchrist's "The Master and his Emissary". The title comes from a fable – possibly by Nietzsche, though maybe not – which McGilchrist describes as follows: "There was once a wise spiritual master, who was the ruler of a small but prosperous domain, and who was known for his selfless devotion to his people. As his people flourished and grew in number, the bounds of this small domain spread; and with it the need to trust implicitly the emissaries he sent to ensure the safety of its ever more distant parts. It was not just that it was impossible for him personally to order all that needed to be dealt with: as he wisely saw, he needed to keep his distance from, and remain ignorant of, such concerns. And, so, he nurtured and trained carefully his emissaries, in order that they could be trusted. Eventually, however, his cleverest and most ambitious vizier, the one he most trusted to do his work, began to see himself as the master, and used his position to advance his own wealth and influence. He saw his master's temperance and forbearance as weakness, not wisdom, and on his missions on the master's behalf, adopted his mantle as his own – the emissary became contemptuous of his master. And so it came about that the master was usurped, the people were duped, the domain became a tyranny; and eventually it collapsed in ruins."

As a way of understanding the problems currently facing us both as individuals and also our whole Western culture over the past 500 years, McGilchrist takes this story as a metaphor for how the two hemispheres of the brain are currently in a state of conflict rather than co-operation. In his view, the right hemisphere – the hemisphere which sees the whole, sees "what is", the one that is comfortable with uncertainty and complexity and ambiguity, the one that values wisdom and uniqueness, the one that favours the living and the embodied, the one "that believes but does not know" – this represents The Master. The left hemisphere, on the other hand – the one which focuses on utility and getting, that likes to grasp and control and manipulate the world, the one that prefers how things "should be", the one that favours the material and the mechanistic, the one that likes to simplify, that craves certainty and clarity, the one "that knows but doesn't believe" – this can be seen as the Emissary.

As I've said repeatedly in previous essays, both hemispheres are essential. They allow us to attend to the world in two very different, opposing ways that ensure our well-being and survival. The two hemispheres complement each other. But – and it's an important "but" – complementarity is not the same as equality.

The left hemisphere has given our civilisation so much. We live longer, we're healthier, richer, safer, better educated than we ever were in past centuries. As a result of technological advancements our lives have improved immeasurably. The left hemisphere can be an extraordinary force for good and achievement. I am in no way being critical of it. In fact, just the opposite. It's precisely because it is so important that it must find its proper place. The left hemisphere is at its best when it is in a supporting role, when it's the emissary. But it is not a good Master. Why? Because it sees so little of the picture. Its desire and ability to focus makes it blind to most of "what is". At the same time, its certainty and self-belief in its own powers means it doesn't realise that there is so much more to see: it doesn't know what it doesn't know. And, convinced of its own importance, it comes to imagine that what it does is more highly evolved than what the right hemisphere does. And so eventually it comes to believe its own hype and propaganda. And that's dangerous.

Whilst we have clearly gained much from our left hemispheres, there's a growing recognition that the "left hemisphere bias" we see around us in our organisations and institutions has come at quite a price. Notwithstanding all the material benefits that we now enjoy, it would be hard to argue that, as a society, we are any wiser than our predecessors. Increasingly there is a sense that en-route to our current position we have lost something important, actually much of what it is that makes us human, what it is that makes life meaningful. Sometimes it can be difficult to articulate what it is that we've lost, what it is that's missing, simply because it's those intangibles associated with the "inarticulate" right hemisphere – a desire for wholeness, aliveness, vibrancy, relationship, connection, co-operation, quality, beauty, humanity. But just because they are hard to pin down or define or measure doesn't make them any less important. They are vital to our lives.

In a New York Times article in 1946 Albert Einstein was quoted as saying: "A new type of thinking is essential if mankind is to survive and move toward higher levels." At that time he was reacting to the recent development and use of atomic weapons, perhaps one of the greatest "achievements" of our technological left hemispheres. If Einstein had still been around in the 21st century he might well have said the same following the economic meltdown of 2008, or in response to the environmental catastrophe we're currently facing. It's clear that we need to think differently, that our attitudes and approaches are no longer working and are past their sell-by dates. Sadly, seventy years on from that Einstein quote, it is hard to discern any real change of mindset in the mainstream.

But 'twas ever thus. To paraphrase Max Planck "Science progresses one funeral at a time. A new scientific truth does not triumph by convincing its opponents and making them see the light, but rather because its opponents eventually die, and a new generation grows up that is familiar with it." So, yes, progress can seem glacially slow. But the upside of Max Planck's view is that we just need to be patient. The dinosaurs will die out.

Whilst there is uncertainty everywhere – environmentally, economically, politically, socially – and whilst these are undoubtedly turbulent and painful times, equally, there is hope. For a start, this turbulence is entirely of our own making and so to quote, once again, Satish Kumar ... "What is created by humans can be changed by humans". If we want our organisations and their values to be different, if we want the behaviours of our employees to be different – be they on the shop floor or in the Boardroom – if we want our Leadership to be different, then we can make it happen. Or more precisely we can let it happen. We can allow these new, developing trends to bubble up and emerge.

Ever more people are questioning "What matters?", not only outside of their work but also within, within their lives as a whole. There are numerous movements away from "the old" and towards "the new". Our Millenials and Post-Millenials – ie: Max Planck's "new generation" – have grown up with a different mindset. And they're moving towards those organisations that they believe will allow "What matters?" to emerge.

As Frederic Laloux observes "The pain we currently feel is the pain of something old that is dying ... while something new is waiting to be born."

Isn't that reason to be deeply hopeful?

Further recommended reading

The Master and his Emissary – Iain McGilchrist
If you hadn't already guessed it, "The Master" is my bible, my Desert-Island book. If you read no other book in your life then you should read this one. It will change you. You will not be the same person afterwards. It is a stunning tour-de-force which ranges across neurology, psychology, psychiatry, science, philosophy, literature, history, and the arts, all the time helping us ponder the fundamental question "What does it mean to be human?". It is a masterpiece.

Rethinking Leadership – Donna Ladkin
Finding a new approach to studying and writing about Leadership is a real challenge – it's a well-worn path – but Donna Ladkin has managed it supremely well. This book is fresh, full of insight, and stimulating. But crucially, it's also beautifully written.

The Answer to How is Yes – Peter Block
This enigmatically-titled volume is a wonderfully thought-provoking guide which helps us question what matters, what's significant to us, what makes our lives meaningful, what we value. And, once we've considered these things, it then helps us reflect on the importance of bringing them into our corporate landscape.

Reinventing Organisations – Frederic Laloux
If you want to hear about "Next-stage" organisations, if you want help in shifting your organisational conversations from "What's broken" to "What's possible", if you want to be inspired by stories of companies that have found ways to be truly powerful, soulful and purposeful, if you want to imagine a new future for your own organisation, then this is the book to read. It will give you hope.

Maestro: Leading by Listening – Roger Nierenberg

If you want to have a visceral first-hand experience of what it means to lead a group of temperamental specialists, and see how it's possible to draw a unified response from them within moments then I urge you to attend one of Roger Nierenberg's "The Music Paradigm" workshops, where attendees sit amongst the orchestral players and get "up close and personal" with real leadership. The next best alternative is to buy and read this delightful fable which distils the learnings from his 20 years of running these sessions.

Jung: A Very Short Introduction – Anthony Stevens

If you want to understand people – your colleagues, your clients, your boss – then for many, Carl Jung is the guide of choice. Unfortunately, Jung wrote mainly for professional psychologists rather than the layman, and so the best way in is to read books not actually by Jung himself but, instead, by others. This slim volume is as good as they come: brilliantly written and extremely readable.

Organizational Learning at NASA – Julianne Mahler
Failure to Learn – Andrew Hopkins

Both of these technical books are about failures in leadership in High Hazard industries, and are vivid but sobering accounts of the two Space Shuttle disasters and the BP Texas City Refinery disaster. If you want examples of what can go wrong when we don't communicate, when we don't listen, when we don't focus on "What Is", and when those people in positions of authority only want to hear "Good News", then look no further. Highly recommended.

Encyclopedia of Positive Questions – Diana Whitney et al

I am a firm believer that asking positive questions brings out the best in people and organisations. If you want to change your world then you must first change your way of asking questions. This powerful little book will give you so many ideas about how you can use Appreciative Inquiry to help you improve Collaboration, Customer service, Teamwork, Leadership, Learning & Development, High Performance, CSR, Employee engagement, Strategic planning. It's a Gold mine.

The Author

Charles Grimes is a Business Psychologist who works with individuals and teams to help them reach their potential.

He qualified initially as a Chartered Surveyor and was a member of the RICS for more than 20 years. He has also worked in classical music Broadcasting for Radio Television Hong Kong. In the late 1990s he re-trained and since then has been consulting with many well known global brands – Allen & Overy, Barclays, British Airways, BP, Clifford Chance, GlaxoSmithKline, Google, Lloyds Bank, McDonalds, Pfizer, Tesco, Unilever, Virgin Atlantic – on the broad subject of Leadership.

He holds an MSc from Ashridge Business School, has taught on the Advanced Management Programme at Henley Business School, has been an Associate Course Director for The Leadership Trust, is a faculty member of the Allen & Overy Smart Start programme, and since 2006 has been a Faculty member of the LBCambridge Spring & Summer Schools for In-house Lawyers held at Queens' College, Cambridge.

He has a strong interest in music – he sings regularly in Hereford Cathedral – and is a Fellow of the Royal Society of Arts. He also has a Private Pilot's Licence and (in his spare time) has run workshops on Banking Reform and Modern Monetary Theory.

He can be contacted via his website: www.CharlesGrimes.com

Lightning Source UK Ltd.
Milton Keynes UK
UKHW021818310322
400910UK00005B/150